American Decades
U·X·L
1960·1969

Tom Pendergast
& Sara Pendergast,
Editors

Detroit • New York • San Diego • San Francisco • Cleveland • New Haven, Conn. • Waterville, Maine • London • Munich

U•X•L American Decades, 1960–1969

Tom Pendergast and Sara Pendergast, Editors

Project Editors
Diane Sawinski, Julie L. Carnagie, and Christine Slovey

Editorial
Elizabeth Anderson

Permissions
Shalice Shah-Caldwell

Imaging and Multimedia
Dean Dauphinais

Product Design
Pamela A.E. Galbreath

Composition
Evi Seoud

Manufacturing
Rita Wimberley

For permission to use material from this product, submit your request via Web at http://www.gale-edit.com/permissions, or you may download our Permissions Request form and submit your request by fax or mail to:

Permissions Department
The Gale Group, Inc.
27500 Drake Rd.
Farmington Hills, MI 48331-3535
Permissions Hotline:
248-699-8006 or 800-877-4253, ext. 8006
Fax: 248-699-8074 or 800-762-4058

Cover photograph reproduced by permission of the Corbis Corporation.

While every effort has been made to ensure the reliability of the information presented in this publication, The Gale Group, Inc. does not guarantee the accuracy of the data contained herein. The Gale Group, Inc. accepts no payment for listing; and inclusion in the publication of any organization, agency, institution, publication, service, or individual does not imply endorsement of the editors or publisher. Errors brought to the attention of the publisher and verified to the satisfaction of the publisher will be corrected in future editions.

Vol. 1: 0-7876-6455-3
Vol. 2: 0-7876-6456-1
Vol. 3: 0-7876-6457-X
Vol. 4: 0-7876-6458-8
Vol. 5: 0-7876-6459-6
Vol. 6: 0-7876-6460-X
Vol. 7: 0-7876-6461-8
Vol. 8: 0-7876-6462-6
Vol. 9: 0-7876-6463-4
Vol. 10: 0-7876-6464-2

LIBRARY OF CONGRESS CATALOGING-IN-PUBLICATION DATA

U•X•L American decades
    p. cm.
Includes bibliographical references and index.
    Contents: v. 1. 1900-1910—v. 2. 1910-1919—v. 3.1920-1929—v. 4. 1930-1939—v. 5. 1940-1949—v. 6. 1950-1959—v. 7. 1960-1969—v. 8. 1970-1979—v. 9.1980-1989—v. 10. 1990-1999.
    Summary: A ten-volume overview of the twentieth century which explores such topics as the arts, economy, education, government, politics, fashions, health, science, technology, and sports which characterize each decade.
    ISBN 0-7876-6454-5 (set: hardcover: alk. paper)
    1. United States—Civilization—20th century—Juvenile literature. 2. United States—History—20th century—Juvenile literature. [1. United States—Civilization—20th century. 2. United States—History—20th century.] I. UXL (Firm) II. Title: UXL American decades. III. Title: American decades.
E169.1.U88 2003
973.91—dc21
2002010176

Contents

Reader's Guide

U•X•L American Decades provides a broad overview of the major events and people that helped to shape American society throughout the twentieth century. Each volume in this ten-volume set chronicles a single decade and begins with an introduction to that decade and a timeline of major events in twentieth-century America. Following are eight chapters devoted to these categories of American endeavor:

• Arts and Entertainment

• Business and the Economy

• Education

• Government, Politics, and Law

• Lifestyles and Social Trends

• Medicine and Health

• Science and Technology

• Sports

These chapters are then divided into five sections:

Chronology: A timeline of significant events within the chapter's particular field.

Overview: A summary of the events and people detailed in that chapter.

Headline Makers: Short biographical accounts of key people and their achievements during the decade.

❖ **Topics in the News:** A series of short topical essays describing events and people within the chapter's theme.

➕ **For More Information:** A section that lists books and Web sites directing the student to further information about the events and people covered in the chapter.

OTHER FEATURES

Each volume of *U•X•L American Decades* contains more than eighty black-and-white photographs and illustrations that bring the events and people discussed to life and sidebar boxes that expand on items of high interest to readers. Concluding each volume is a general bibliography of books and Web sites that explore the particular decade in general and a thorough subject index that allows readers to easily locate the events, people, and places discussed throughout that volume of *U•X•L American Decades*.

COMMENTS AND SUGGESTIONS

We welcome your comments on *U•X•L American Decades* and suggestions for other history topics to consider. Please write: Editors, *U•X•L American Decades*, U•X•L, 27500 Drake Rd., Farmington Hills, MI 48331-3535; call toll-free: 1-800-877-4253; fax: 248-699-8097; or send e-mail via http://www.galegroup.com.

Chronology of the 1960s

1960:   The USS *George Washington,* a state of the art nuclear-powered submarine, is launched.

1960:   **February 1** Students stage a sit-in at a "whites-only" lunch counter in Greensboro, North Carolina.

1960:   **April** A breast implant is constructed from silicone gel.

1960:   **April 1** *Tiros 1,* the first weather satellite, is launched.

1960:   **May** Birth control pills are approved for widespread use in the United States.

1960:   **May 5** A U-2 spy plane is shot down over Soviet territory, launching a crisis between the United States and Soviet Union, which results in the cancellation of a U.S.-Russian summit meeting.

1960:   **May 6** The 1960 Civil Rights Act becomes law.

1960:   **September** "The Twist," a pop song recorded by Chubby Checker, hits the number one spot on the *Billboard* Top 40 charts.

1960:   **September 26** Presidential nominees Democrat John F. Kennedy and Republican Richard M. Nixon meet for the first-ever televised debate between presidential candidates.

1961:   Texas Instruments patents the first silicon chip used for electronic circuits.

1961:   The President's Commission on the Status of Women is formed to study the legal and economic rights of women.

1961: Yo-yos become a national toy craze.

1961: **January 3** The U.S. breaks diplomatic relations with Cuba.

1961: **January 10** Two black students register at the University of Georgia. Consequent riots lead to their suspension; however, school administrators are ordered to reinstate them.

1961: **February 15** The entire U.S. figure-skating team is killed in a plane crash while traveling to the world championships in Prague, Czechoslovakia.

1961: **April** Folk singer Bob Dylan makes his debut at Gerde's Folk City in Greenwich Village, New York.

1961: **May 4** The Freedom Riders begin traveling throughout the American South to counteract racism and segregation.

1961: **May 5** Astronaut Alan B. Shepard Jr. becomes the first American launched into space.

1961: **May 5** President John F. Kennedy signs the Fair Labor Standards Act, increasing the minimum wage from $1 to $1.25 by September 1963.

1961: **May 21–22** A bus carrying Freedom Riders is attacked by an angry mob in Montgomery, Alabama.

1961: **October 1** Roger Maris hits his sixty-first home run, breaking the record held by Babe Ruth since 1927.

1962: Radiation, chemotherapy, and steroids are used to fight leukemia.

1962: A televised tour shows First Lady Jacqueline Kennedy's redecoration of the White House, which she completed under the supervision of the National Fine Arts Commission.

1962: **March 1** In the largest antitrust case to date, a federal district court orders E. I. Du Pont de Nemours and Company to divest itself of 63 million shares of General Motors stock.

1962: **May 28** In the single greatest daily loss since 1929, the New York Stock Exchange plummets by nearly $21 billion. Fortunately, stocks quickly rebound.

1962: **June 25** The U.S. Supreme Court rules unconstitutional a prayer reading in New York public schools.

1962: **July 27** A price-fixing scandal ends with General Electric consenting to pay $7.5 million in damages for excess profits.

1962: **August 5** Actress Marilyn Monroe dies from an overdose of barbiturates.

1962: **August 31** Due to threats of violence, Roman Catholic Church officials close an integrated parochial school in Buras, Mississippi.

1962: **September 15** To stimulate projects in economically depressed regions, President Kennedy signs into law a $900 million public works bill.

1962: **September 20** In defiance of a federal court order, James Meredith, a black man, is denied admission to the University of Mississippi. Ten days later, Meredith is escorted onto the "Ole Miss" campus. After fifteen hours of shooting and rioting in which two persons are killed, Meredith is enrolled.

1962: **October 22** President Kennedy announces the presence of Soviet missiles in Cuba. The resulting crisis ends one week later.

1963: **January 28** Harvey Gantt becomes the first black student at South Carolina's Clemson College.

1963: **April 13** Cincinnati Reds rookie Pete Rose smacks his first major league hit.

1963: **June 11** After threatening to defy a federal desegregation mandate, Governor George C. Wallace allows two black students to enroll at the University of Alabama.

1963: **July 25** The United States, Soviet Union, and Great Britain sign the Partial Nuclear Test Ban Treaty.

1963: **August 18** James Meredith becomes the first black Bachelors degree candidate at the University of Mississippi.

1963: **September 15** Four little girls are killed when a black Birmingham, Alabama, church is bombed.

1963: **November 22** President Kennedy is assassinated in Dallas, Texas. Vice President Lyndon Johnson becomes the new chief executive.

1963: **November 24** The murder of alleged presidential assassin Lee Harvey Oswald is broadcast live on television.

1964: The Verrazano Narrows Bridge, the world's largest suspension bridge, opens in New York City.

1964: IBM produces a new product, the word processor, a hybrid of the typewriter and computer.

1964: **January 8** In his State of the Union message, President Johnson declares a "War on Poverty."

1964: **February 9** The Beatles make their first appearance on American television, on *The Ed Sullivan Show* (1948–71).

1964: **February 25** Cassius Clay, who would change his name to Muhammed Ali a month later, wins the heavyweight boxing crown from Sonny Liston.

1964: **February 26** The Tax Reduction Act lowers personal and corporate income tax rates.

1964: **April** The one-hundred-billionth Bayer aspirin tablet is produced.

1964: **April 17** The Ford Motor Company unveils its new Mustang.

1964: **June 24** The Federal Trade Commission (FTC) proclaims that, beginning in 1965, cigarette packaging must feature health warnings.

1964: **July 2** The Civil Rights Act of 1964 becomes law.

1964: **July 18** Riots break out in New York City's Harlem and Brownsville and spread to other cities.

1964: **September–December** University of California at Berkeley students demonstrate against a ban on on-campus free speech. The protest culminates in a student strike.

1964: **September 25** The United Auto Workers strike General Motors. A contract agreement is reached two weeks later, but local strikers hinder production for another month.

1964: **September 28** The Warren Commission reports that Lee Harvey Oswald acted alone in killing President Kennedy.

1964: **September 30** President Johnson signs the Equal Opportunity Act, providing funding for youth programs, antipoverty measures, and small business loans.

1965: The U.S. Congress passes the Motor Vehicle Air Pollution Act.

1965: **February 21** Black nationalist leader Malcolm X is assassinated.

1965: **March 5** The Freedom School, an integrated school in Indianola, Mississippi, is burned to the ground.

1965: **March 7** State and local police attack civil rights marchers in Selma, Alabama.

1965: **April 9** The Houston Astrodome, an enclosed air-conditioned stadium 642 feet in diameter, opens.

1965: **June 8** President Johnson authorizes American troops to engage in direct combat operations in Vietnam.

1965: **July 15** *Mariner 4* sends the first close-up photographs of Mars.

1965: **August 6** The 1965 Voting Rights Act becomes law.

1965: **August 11** Large-scale riots break out in Watts, a black Los Angeles, California, neighborhood.

1965: **September 25** Fifty-nine-year-old baseball legend Satchel Paige pitches three scoreless innings for the Kansas City A's.

1966: The Black Panther Party is organized.

1966: **January** Kentucky becomes the first southern state to pass a civil rights law.

1966: **February 27** Seventeen-year-old Peggy Fleming, three-time U.S. champion, wins the world figure-skating championship.

1966: **March 3** President Johnson signs into law the Veteran's Readjustment Act, allowing education benefits for those who served in the military after January 31, 1955.

1966: **March 12** Bobby Hull becomes the first National Hockey League (NHL) player to score fifty goals in a season.

1966: **April 11** Jack Nicklaus becomes the first golfer to win two straight Masters titles.

1966: **July 1** The Medicare health insurance plan for Americans over sixty-five-years-old is instituted.

1966: **September 9** President Johnson signs into law the Traffic Safety Act, establishing safety standards for automobiles.

1966: **October** Betty Friedan is elected the first president of the National Organization for Women (NOW).

1966: **December 2** U.S. Roman Catholics no longer are required to abstain from eating meat on Fridays, except during Lent.

1967: A cordless, battery-powered telephone is developed.

1967: A solar-powered house is built.

1967: To counter the popularity of the Ford Mustang, Chevrolet introduces the two-seat Camaro SS.

1967: **January 27** A launch pad fire kills American astronauts Virgil "Gus" Grissom, Edward H. White, and Roger B. Chaffee during a test for what would have been the first space mission with a three-person crew on board.

1967: **March 1** The first overseas direct telephone dialing begins.

1967: **June 20** Muhammad Ali is stripped of his title as heavyweight boxing champion for refusing military service on religious grounds and to protest continued military action in Vietnam.

1967: **July 23–30** Race riots in Detroit leave forty-three dead.

1967: **November 9** The first issue of *Rolling Stone* magazine is published. A portrait of the Beatles's John Lennon is featured on the cover.

1967: **December** Christiaan Barnard performs the first human-to-human heart transplant operation.

1967: **December** Universal News, the last of the movie newsreel companies, closes because it is unable to compete with television news.

1968: The 100-story John Hancock Building in Chicago becomes the world's tallest building.

1968: **January 15** The Supreme Court approves a New York Central/Pennsylvania railroads merger, creating the country's largest railroad.

1968: **April 4** Martin Luther King Jr. is assassinated in Memphis, Tennessee.

1968: **April 11** The Civil Rights Act of 1968 becomes law.

1968: **June 4** U.S. Attorney General Robert Kennedy is assassinated.

1968: **June 13** The New York Stock Exchange sets a record with 2,350,000 shares exchanged in one day.

1968: **August** Police battle protesters outside the Democratic National Convention in Chicago.

1968: **September 9** Arthur Ashe becomes the first African American to win the U.S. Open Tennis Tournament.

1968: **November 1** The Motion Picture Association of America inaugurates its film ratings system.

1968: **November 14** Yale University admits women.

1969: **May 7** Seven are injured in a confrontation between black and white students at New York's City College.

1969: **July 16** *Apollo 11* is launched. This flight culminates in the landing of the first human on the surface of the moon, on July 19.

1969:   **August 15–17** The Woodstock Music and Art Fair is held on a 600-acre hog farm in Upstate New York.

1969:   **November 20** The Department of Agriculture announces plans to phase out use of the pesticide DDT (dichlorodiphenyltrichloroethane) because of its health and environmental hazards.

The 1960s: An Overview

The 1960s was a time of enormous cultural and political upheaval in the United States. The decade's most infamous date is November 22, 1963. That day, U.S. president John F. Kennedy (1917–1963) was assassinated. His murder was followed by those of other national figures, including civil rights leaders Martin Luther King Jr. (1929–1968) and Malcolm X (1925–1965), and presidential candidate and brother of President Kennedy, Robert Kennedy (1925–1968). The movement for equality for black Americans, which began during previous decades, fully escalated during the 1960s. It was not an easy fight, as Southern hard-liners and racists resisted attempts to integrate schools and allow blacks the right to vote. Occasionally, civil rights workers were met with beatings and even bullets.

At the same time, the United States and the Soviet Union were immersed in the cold war, an ideological struggle that pitted democracy against communism. Occasionally, this conflict threatened to escalate into nuclear war. The most notorious instance was the 1962 Cuban Missile Crisis, during which the Soviet Union endeavored to install nuclear weapons in Cuba within striking distance of the United States. Another attempt to halt the spread of communism, this one in Southeast Asia, was bloody and controversial. During mid-decade, President Lyndon Johnson (1908–1973) began increasing the number of American troops in Vietnam. With each passing year, as more and more troops were sent to Vietnam, antiwar protests grew larger and louder. In the end, Johnson's Vietnam policy, which was doomed to failure, far overshadowed his other policies, especially his attempt to appropriate federal money into the creation of a "Great Society," in which poverty and blight in America would be eradicated. Johnson's plan for the country never was fulfilled, however.

American corporations increasingly merged during the decade, creating larger and more powerful conglomerates. Discount chain stores and fast-food restaurants replaced family-owned businesses. Small farms were becoming extinct and were replaced by larger, often corporate-owned entities. Manufacturing jobs were being relocated from the Northeast to nonunion Southern states and foreign countries. On a more upbeat note, the economy generally flourished. The development of silicon chips and integrated computer circuits resulted in an electronics revolution and the dawn of the Information Age.

Progress also was made on the medical and scientific fronts during the decade. Wonder drugs alleviated and cured diseases. Limb reattachments and liver, lung, and heart transplants were successfully performed. Efforts also were made to develop an artificial heart. Satellites circled Earth, recording weather patterns and relaying live television signals. Astronauts from the United States and cosmonauts from the Soviet Union rode rockets into space. By decade's end, Americans had landed on the Moon.

But the 1960s triumphs were obscured by the turmoil of the era. Pop art, the principal art movement of the decade, grew from the concept that American consumer culture was so trite that it might as well be regarded as art. A youth culture emerged, in response to what young people viewed as the wasteland of middle-class materialism. As Baby Boomers, the children of the World War II generation, came of age, many became political activists. Young people, especially those enrolled in college, demonstrated for civil rights and against the Vietnam War. They openly criticized the policies of Lyndon Johnson and his successor, Richard M. Nixon (1913–1994). They were tear-gassed as they clashed with Chicago police during the 1968 Democratic National Convention. They experimented with sex and drugs. Between four hundred thousand and five hundred thousand of them were serenaded by an all-star roster of rock performers one rain-soaked weekend in 1969 at the Woodstock Music and Art Fair. Women embraced the concept that they should be afforded the same economic and social opportunities as men, and a new feminist revolution was born. The cult heroes of the young were neither cosmetically pretty movie stars nor political leaders from the dusty pages of history books. They were cutting-edge rock performers and maverick moviemakers. The Beatles, a mop-topped quartet of musicians who hailed from Liverpool, England, altered the face of popular culture. The evolution of their music mirrored the vast changes occurring among young people. Folk-rock singer and composer Bob Dylan (1941–) was a poet and prophet of the era. The title of one of his most famous compositions reflects the tenor of the 1960s: "The Times They Are A-Changin."

Arts and Entertainment

1960: **January 3** The Moscow State Symphony begins a seven-week tour at New York's Carnegie Hall, becoming the first Soviet orchestra to perform in the United States.

1960: **February 11** Jack Paar, host of *The Tonight Show,* walks off the show when an NBC censor deletes a joke from his performance.

1960: **April** The New York State legislature authorizes the city of New York to purchase Carnegie Hall, which was scheduled for demolition.

1960: **April 1** Lucille Ball and Desi Arnaz appear for the last time as Lucy and Ricky Ricardo on *The Lucy-Desi Comedy Hour* (1957–60).

1960: **October 13** Jazz trumpeter Louis Armstrong begins a goodwill tour of Africa, partially sponsored by the U.S. State Department.

1961: **January 20** Robert Frost reads his poem "The Gift Outright" at the inauguration of President John F. Kennedy.

1961: **January 27** Soprano Leontyne Price first performs at New York's Metropolitan Opera.

1961: **April** Folk singer Bob Dylan makes his debut at Gerde's Folk City in Greenwich Village, New York.

1962: **May 30** Jazz clarinetist Benny Goodman begins a six-week, U.S. State Department-arranged tour of Russia.

1962: **August 5** Actress Marilyn Monroe dies from an overdose of barbiturates.

1962: **September 25** Philharmonic Hall, the first completed building of New York's Lincoln Center for the Performing Arts, is inaugurated by Leonard Bernstein and the New York Philharmonic.

1963: **January 8** *Mona Lisa,* by Leonardo da Vinci, is shown at Washington's National Gallery, the first time the painting ever has appeared outside the Louvre in Paris.

1963: **May 7** The Guthrie Theatre in Minneapolis, the first major regional theater in the Midwest, opens.

1963: **November 24** The murder of alleged presidential assassin Lee Harvey Oswald is broadcast live on television.

1964: **February 9** The Beatles make their first appearance on American televi-

sion, on *The Ed Sullivan Show*
(1948–71).

1964: **May** The just-remodeled Museum of
Modern Art in New York City reopens
with a new gallery, the Steichen Pho-
tography Center, named for photogra-
pher Edward Steichen.

1965: **April 26** *Symphony No. 4* (1916) by
Charles Ives is performed in its entire-
ty for the first time by the American
Symphony Orchestra, conducted by
Leopold Stokowski.

1965: **May 9** Piano virtuoso Vladimir
Horowitz returns to the Carnegie Hall
stage after a twelve-year-long "retire-
ment."

1965: **September 29** President Lyndon
Johnson signs into the law the Federal Aid to the Arts Bill.

1966: **August 29** The Beatles play their last
live concert.

1967: **February 18** The National Gallery of
Art arranges to purchase da Vinci's
Ginevra dei Benci for between $5 and
$6 million, the highest price paid to
date for a single painting.

1967: **June** The Monterey International Pop
Festival, an important early rock
music event, is held in California.

1967: **November 9** The first issue of *Rolling
Stone* magazine is published. A portrait of The Beatles' John Lennon is
featured on the cover.

1967: **December** Universal News, the last
of the movie newsreel companies,
closes because it is unable to compete with television news.

1968: **April 19** *Hair* opens on Broadway, at
the Biltmore Theatre.

1968: **September 16** Presidential candidate
Richard M. Nixon appears as a guest
on TV's *Rowan and Martin's Laugh-In*
(1968–73) and delivers one of the
show's signature lines: "Sock it to me."

1968: **November 1** The Motion Picture
Association of America inaugurates
its film ratings system.

1969: **August 15–17** The Woodstock Music
and Art Fair is held on a 600-acre hog
farm in upstate New York.

❋ *Overview*

The 1960s were a decade of political and social turmoil marked by the assassinations of several prominent political leaders, the expansion of the Civil Rights movement, and violent protests against the war in Vietnam. Young people played a leading role in the movements to influence politics and culture. Not surprisingly, the views and lifestyles of young people also had a great influence on the popular arts. There were still countless films, books, and plays that reflected the interests of middle-class adults and contained formulaic characters, predictable story lines, and warm and fuzzy happy endings. But a new breed of cutting-edge films, books, and plays proved to be more than disposable brain candy; they were bold, irreverent, and adventurous. They reflected the cynicism and alienation that characterized the younger generations in the 1960s by depicting characters who challenged or even mocked authority.

The characters depicted in these new works included such unconventional heroes, as a spunky mental patient who is saner than the oppressive authority figures who control his fate (in Ken Kesey's novel, *One Flew Over the Cuckoo's Nest*); a pair of motorcyclists who set out in search of America and find only racism and violence (in the movie *Easy Rider*); a college-educated young man who looks at his elders and sees only artificial values and hypocrisy (in the film *The Graduate*); a band of hippie-types who strip off their clothes to celebrate the dawning of a liberated age they called the Age of Aquarius (in the stage play *Hair*); and a World War II-era aviator who yearns for peace but is caught in a frustrating, illogical paradox (in Joseph Heller's novel, *Catch 22*).

Even television, by now the most mainstream of all media, occasionally emitted bursts of creativity while appealing directly to the sensibilities of the young. But for the most part, much of what viewers saw when they clicked on their sets was bland and unimaginative: lowbrow programs inhabiting what Federal Communications Commission chairman Newton Minow called "a vast wasteland" in a 1961 speech.

Pop Art, the decade's prevailing art movement, took the objects and images of consumer culture and elevated them to the status of art. The designs and logos of commercial packaging became the subject of artists' work, as did stylized images of pop culture icons like Marilyn Monroe. The "new" art both celebrated and critiqued popular culture.

In the motion picture industry, a generation of young filmmakers and stars emerged who produced films that were exciting and innovative, and that appealed to the baby boomers. The Production Code, which for decades had dictated the content of movies, fell by the wayside. The result: films became more graphically violent, dialogue became more raw and realistic, and on-screen nudity was no longer against the rules.

The music favored by the young was loud and liberating, but it also could be soulful and stirring. If at the beginning of the decade such music reflected romantic, idealistic teenaged dreams, by the end it had matured along with its audience and reflected a range of issues, emotions, and experiences, mirroring the growing political consciousness of the younger generations in this decade.

A sampling of names and phrases synonymous with the era include the rock festival Woodstock and the pop artist Andy Warhol; rock music icons The Beatles and The Rolling Stones; *Easy Rider* actors Dennis Hopper and Peter Fonda; and catch phrases like "sock it to me" and, most prophetically, "the times they are a-changin'," the latter from a song by folk rock pioneer Bob Dylan.

The Beatles John Lennon (1940–1980); Paul McCartney (1942–); George Harrison (1943–2001); Ringo Starr (1940–) In 1964, The Beatles burst onto the music scene and not only became international celebrities but altered the face of music and popular culture. Their music, a combination of pop and rock and roll, reflected the development of rock music throughout the decade, moving from sweet and innocent in 1964 to hard-edged and psychedelic by the end of the decade. Their phenomenal success was dubbed Beatlemania. As the decade progressed, the members of The Beatles evolved both musically and personally. In 1970, they disbanded the group, citing personal and artistic conflicts. *Photo reproduced by permission of the Corbis Corporation.*

Johnny Carson (1925–) Johnny Carson took over NBC's late-night program *The Tonight Show* from previous host, Jack Paar in 1957, and turned it into a television institution during the 1960s. Carson was able to far outpace all other competing shows in the ratings due to his comedic talents and his ability to attract celebrity guests to his show. Because of *The Tonight Show's* popularity, sponsors' revenues for the program reached $20 million in 1967, a $4 million increase over the highest billings during Paar's years. Carson remained host until retiring in 1992. *Photo reproduced by permission of Archive Photos, Inc.*

Walter Cronkite (1916–) During the 1960s, Walter Cronkite was the most respected television newscaster in the United States. The longtime anchor of CBS's nightly news broadcast, Cronkite presided over the decade's most tumultuous events, from the assassination of President John F. Kennedy (1917–1963) to the Apollo 11 moon landing. Cronkite's demeanor and integrity made him the nation's father figure. His on-the-air conversion from Vietnam War supporter to questioner of American foreign policy helped sway the American public's viewpoint of the war. *Photo reproduced courtesy of the Library of Congress.*

Bob Dylan (1941–) Bob Dylan was a poet/prophet of the early 1960s. He started out as a humanist-oriented folksinger whose primary influence was Woody Guthrie (1912–1967), the fabled Depression-era Dust Bowl balladeer. However, Dylan's music came to reflect the decade's social unrest. In his early folk compositions, he lampooned segregation, denounced the purveyors of nuclear weapons, and pronounced, for all the world to hear, "The Times They Are a-Changin'." Dylan changed folk music forever when, in 1965, he set aside his acoustic guitar, picked up an electric one, and transformed himself into a rock star. *Photo reproduced by permission of AP/Wide World Photos.*

Sidney Poitier (1927–) Sidney Poitier contributed to promoting a positive image of blacks through his acting roles during the 1960s. He was the first black leading man in Hollywood, and the first to win an Academy Award for Best Actor for his performance in the 1963 film *Lilies of the Field.* In this film, Poitier was invariably cast as a responsible role model for blacks and whites alike. Poitier's most active year was 1967 with two important roles: *In the Heat of the Night* and *Guess Who's Coming to Dinner?* Poitier's friendly, hard-working characters comforted many filmgoers, especially whites, during a decade of social unrest. *Photo reproduced courtesy of the Library of Congress.*

Barbra Streisand (1942–) Barbra Streisand, a premier singer and actor of stage and screen, conquered the American musical stage by playing comedienne Fanny Brice (1891–1961) in *Funny Girl,* which came to Broadway in 1964. In 1963 she won two Grammy awards for the first of several top-selling record albums. She won a Best Actress Academy Award in her film debut, the screen adaptation of *Funny Girl* (1968). In future decades, she added film producing and directing to her accomplishments, and she continued to enjoy success as a recording artist. *Photo reproduced by permission of Archive Photos, Inc.*

Andy Warhol (1930–1987) During the 1960s, Andy Warhol and American art were one and the same. He was the era's leading Pop Artist, reproducing images from popular culture. He also was a cutting edge filmmaker, directing a series of films of varying lengths that were experimental, controversial, and undeniably influential. Warhol was a master self-promoter who is perhaps most famous for his astute declaration that, in our media and celebrity-obsessed culture, everyone eventually will become famous, but only for fifteen minutes. Warhol's own celebrity, however, lasted longer than a quarter-hour. It endures years past his death. *Photo reproduced by permission of AP/Wide World Photos.*

Jann Wenner (1946–) Jann Wenner was among the first entrepreneurs to understand the commercial potential of the emerging Baby Boomer market. In 1967, when he was just twenty-years-old, he borrowed $7,500 and began publishing *Rolling Stone,* a magazine that catered to the era's rock music-oriented youth culture. The content of *Rolling Stone* included a range of subjects, from music reviews to political reporting. It was one of the era's most valuable cultural and political voices. *Photo reproduced by permission of the Corbis Corporation.*

◆ *Topics in the News* . . . .

❖ THE MOVIES GET HIP

The 1960s saw radical changes in the production and content of motion pictures. As the decade began, the studio system (in which major studios controlled the entire production of films) was in its final decline. Fewer films were being made on the Hollywood studio lots; more were being filmed on location. Fewer

*Faye Dunaway and
Warren Beatty as the title
characters in the 1967
film* Bonnie and Clyde.
**Reproduced by permission of
the Kobal Collection.**

Duntring the 1960s, a decline in the power of the Production Code, which previously had determined the content of American movies, resulted in major changes in what could be seen on movie screens. Increasing amounts of nudity, graphic language, and violence were appearing in major motion pictures. To avoid government censorship, the Motion Picture Association of America (MPAA) inaugurated a voluntary ratings system to help guide viewers with regard to movie content. The original MPAA ratings were G (general audiences); M (mature audiences); R (restricted; no one under seventeen admitted without parent or guardian); and X (admission restricted to those over age eighteen).

The assumption was that only products of the sex film industry would earn X ratings, but this was not the case. *Midnight Cowboy* (1969), directed by John Schlesinger (1926–), a searing chronicle of the friendship between two down-and-out losers in seedy New York City, became the first X-rated film to win a Best Picture Academy Award. It had earned its X rating not for nudity, but for its graphic portrayal of sex and violence.

projects were being initiated by the studios themselves; instead, stars and directors were choosing their own projects. Glossy, big-budget productions still proved to be popular. For example, such action-adventure films as *Dr. No* (1962), *From Russia With Love* (1963), and *Goldfinger* (1964), all featuring Sean Connery (1930–) as superspy James Bond, were audience favorites. *The Sound of Music* (1965), a traditionally structured Hollywood musical that offered wholesome family entertainment, was a blockbuster hit. But by decade's end, big-budget genre films consistently would become box office busts, as evidenced by the failures of such lavishly produced musicals as *Star!* (1968) and *Darling Lili* (1970).

Two films in particular captured the imaginations of the young during the decade, and altered the face of moviemaking: *The Graduate* (1967), directed by Mike Nichols (1931–), about an alienated college graduate struggling to find his place in the world; and *Easy Rider* (1969), directed by Dennis Hopper (1936–), charting the exploits of two drug-dealing motorcyclists as they treked across an often hostile America. Both movies featured smallish budgets, young actors (Hopper, Peter Fonda, Jack Nicholson, Dustin Hoffman, and Katharine Ross), and soundtracks loaded with contemporary music (Simon and Garfunkel songs on *The Graduate*, music by The Byrds, Steppenwolf, The Band, Jimi Hendrix, and others on *Easy Rider*). Two other films that resonated among the young were *Bonnie and Clyde* (1967), directed by Arthur Penn (1922–), which portrayed real-life 1930s criminals Bonnie Parker (1910–1934) and Clyde Barrow (1909–1934) as American folk heroes; and *2001: A Space Odyssey* (1968), a landmark science fiction fantasy directed by Stanley Kubrick (1928–1999).

As a result of these successes, Hollywood became more youth-oriented, with a new generation of young filmmakers replacing old-guard moviemakers at the center of Hollywood power. Meanwhile, such nontraditional leading men as Walter Matthau (1920–2000), George C. Scott (1926–1999), and Gene Hackman (1931–), all essentially character actors, became major Hollywood stars.

❖ ROCK AND ROLL REGAINS ITS DANGEROUS EDGE

In the 1960s as in the late 1950s, rock and roll—a new kind of music that was loud and emotional, and rooted in country rockabilly, gospel, rural blues, and urban rhythm and blues—was the most popular music among young people. At the beginning of the decade, however, rock and roll had faded in popularity from its initial surge in the late 1950s and was in a downswing for several reasons. Elvis Presley (1935–1977), the 1950s most acclaimed rock and roller, had entered the United States Army and rising stars Buddy Holly (1936–1959), Ritchie Valens (1941–1959), and J. P Richardson, better known as "The Big Bopper" (1930–1959), had died in a plane crash.

The Elvis who emerged from the military in 1960 had mellowed from the hip-shaking, nostril-flaring sexual icon who had seemed so challenging in 1956 and 1957. In the decade's early years, the pop charts were dominated by such cute but sexually safe teenybopper heartthrobs as Frankie Avalon, Bobby Rydell, Ricky Nelson, Bobby Vee, and Fabian. Top Ten hits included sentimental love songs and variations of 1950s doo-wop and dance music.

Rock and roll may have lost some of its dangerous edge, but this lack of energy was temporary. The music was revived as a major cultural force with what came to be known as the British Invasion. In the mid-1960s, groups of British performers stormed the pop music charts, following the enormous success of The Beatles in 1964. Among them were The Rolling Stones, The Yardbirds, Gerry and The Pacemakers, The Dave Clark Five, Peter and Gordon, and The Animals. At the height of the British Invasion, the common assumption was that the musical sounds emanating from across the sea had originated there. This was not so. At various times, individual British rockers freely acknowledged the influence of such

A range of rock-oriented musical styles enjoyed brief popularity during the 1960s. At the beginning of the decade, the favorite musical styles mostly were pop-oriented and were sweetly innocent. In such songs as "Johnny Angel," "Angel Baby," and "My Guy," love was portrayed as sweet, pure, and simple. Such all-female "girl groups" as The Chiffons, The Shirelles, The Marvelettes, The Shangri-Las, The Ronettes, and The Crystals asked musical questions, such as "Will you still love me tomorrow?" and made musical declarations, like "He's so fine!" and "My boyfriend's back, and you're gonna be in trouble." Meanwhile, West Coast groups such as The Beach Boys celebrated sun, surf, and "California Girls."

As the 1960s came to an end, a cultural revolution had engulfed America's youth. This revolution was reflected in music. Many musical sounds were hard-edged and blatantly drug-related. The Doors sang of being unable to get much higher, while The Jefferson Airplane made knowing references to drug use when they observed that certain pills makes you larger, while others make you small—"and the ones that Mother gives you don't do anything at all."

1950s African American rock and roll legends as Chuck Berry (1926–) and Little Richard (1935–).

The two British groups with the most durability were The Rolling Stones, fronted by their controversial, charismatic lead singer, Mick Jagger (1943–), and The Beatles, a mop-topped quartet whose members were John Lennon (1940–1980), Paul McCartney (1942–), George Harrison (1943–2001), and Ringo Starr (1940–). From the outset, The Rolling Stones were the bad boys. While they were musically suggesting to their female fans, "Let's Spend the Night Together," The Beatles (otherwise known as the Fab Four) were more innocently harmonizing, "I Wanna Hold Your Hand." However The Beatles, personally as well as musically, were to undergo far-reaching changes during the decade, transformations that directly mirrored the evolution of rock and roll. Their sounds progressed from rock and roll-inspired ("She Loves You," "I Wanna Hold Your Hand," "Love Me Do," "Twist and Shout") to artistic, introspective, and hauntingly beautiful ("A Day in the Life," "Yesterday," "Eleanor Rigby"),

Rock Festivals

In the 1960s, the rock festival became a favored venue for music lovers to gather in an outdoor setting and savor the sounds of their preferred performers. A fabled early festival was the 1967 Monterey International Pop Festival, which featured a who's who of rock stars, including Jimi Hendrix, Otis Redding, Janis Joplin, The Who, The Jefferson Airplane, and The Mamas and the Papas. The event was chronicled in *Monterey Pop* (1969), the first important rock concert documentary.

By far the most famous rock festival was the Woodstock Music and Art Fair, held in August 1969. During a rain-soaked three-day weekend, a spirited crowd, numbering between 400,000 and 500,000, converged on a 600-acre hog farm near Bethel, New York. Despite poor planning and general chaos, the crowd remained mellow. The entertainers included an all-star roster of talent, from Country Joe and The Fish, Joe Cocker, Canned Heat, and Crosby, Stills, Nash and Young to Janis Joplin, Jimi Hendrix, and The Who. The event was chronicled in *Woodstock* (1970), an Academy Award-winning documentary.

Unlike Woodstock, however, not all rock festivals were filled with peace and love. The Altamont festival, held in California four months after Woodstock, was an ugly, violent affair during which a festival-goer was murdered.

drug-inspired ("Strawberry Fields," "Lucy in the Sky with Diamonds"), and spiritual ("Love You To," "Let It Be"). The Beatles expanded the boundaries of rock by experimenting with instrumentation, for example George mastered the sitar, which he played on several of The Beatles cuts, as well as orchestration and composition.

Rock music in general followed the trend of The Beatles. From the sweet sincerity of the early part of the decade, rock and roll became harder, darker, and louder. Reflecting the spirit of the age, rock musicians sang about their anger at "The Establishment" and their experimentation with drugs and casual sex. By the end of the decade, rock and roll had not only regained but actually increased its reputation as the music of youthful anger and rebellion.

As the 1950s had closed with the deaths of Holly, Valens, and Richardson, the 1960s also ended with the deaths of three of the decade's rock legends: Janis Joplin (1943–1970), Jimi Hendrix (1942–1970), and Jim Morrison (1943–1971), lead singer of The Doors. However, the difference in the eras is indicated by the manner in which these three expired. Joplin and Hendrix died of drug overdoses. Morrison allegedly was felled by a heart attack, but his well-known habits of drug abuse led to rumors that his death also was drug-related.

❖ THE MOTOWN SOUND

When one thinks of the top African American singers and musicians of the 1960s, one word comes to mind: Motown. Actually, Motown—a shortening of "motortown," a slang name for Detroit, the home of the American automobile industry—first was the name of a record label. It was founded in 1959 by Berry Gordy Jr. (1929–), a songwriter, record producer, and song publisher who hailed from Detroit. Barrett Strong's "Money," The Marvelettes' "Please Mr. Postman," The Miracles' "Shop Around," Mary Wells' "You Beat Me to the Punch," and The Contours' "Do You Love Me" were among the company's first hits. During the 1960s, Motown was phenomenally successful; by mid-decade, it had become the single most profitable black-owned corporation in America. Of the 535 singles issued by Motown during the decade, an astounding 357 were hits. In 1988, Gordy sold Motown to MCA for $61 million.

The Motown sound was distinctive. The songwriting-producing team of Eddie Holland (1939–), Lamont Dozier (1941–), and Brian Holland (1941–), popularly known as Holland/Dozier/Holland, merit much of the credit for its evolution. The best of Motown combined elements of rhythm and blues with gospel; for good reason, it also was known as "soul music." Yet the sounds of Motown also were bouncy and danceable, and they appealed to white as well as black teens. Gordy even concocted a phrase to be used to market his music: "The Sound of Young America."

Among the roster of Motown artists who became superstars and 1960s music legends were The Miracles, who recorded a series of hits after "Shop Around," with lead singer Smokey Robinson (1940–) becoming a model practitioner of the Motown sound. The Temptations were one of the most beloved of all Motown groups; their recording of "My Girl," a special favorite of the era, combined memorably lilting harmonies. Marvin Gaye (1939–1984) was a gospel music-influenced soloist whose top 1960s single was "I Heard It Through the Grapevine," also recorded by Gladys Knight (1944–) and The Pips, another vintage Motown act. Gaye's visionary 1971 album, *What's Going On,* combined massive doses of soul, heart, and humanism.

Little Stevie Wonder (1950–) was just twelve years old when he enjoyed a smash hit with "Fingertips (Part 2)." However, Stevie was no

The Temptations were a popular Motown group who had many hit songs during the 1960s.
Reproduced by permission of Archive Photos, Inc.

one-shot wonder. He matured artistically, dropped the "Little" from his billing, and recorded such hits as "For Once in My Life," "I Was Made to Love Her," and "My Cherie Amour." The Four Tops were fronted by charismatic lead singer Levi Stubbs (1936–); among their most exuberant recordings were "Baby I Need Your Loving," "I Can't Help Myself," and "Reach Out I'll Be There." The Supremes were the prime Motown chart-busters, with "Where Did Our Love Go" becoming the first of their twelve number-one hits. The Supremes' lead singer, Diana Ross (1944–), went on to enjoy a successful career as a soloist. But it was Martha and The Vandel-

Not all the top black singers of the 1960s were affiliated with Motown. Aretha Franklin (1942–), whose background was in gospel music, was perhaps the decade's most electrifying female soloist. Her soul-filled recordings of "Baby I Love You," "Chain of Fools," and, in particular, "Respect" are late-1960s favorites. Franklin's appropriately titled "Lady Soul" is an all-time classic soul music album.

Otis Redding (1941–1967), a dynamic soul singer, was another casualty of the era. He was a rising star when he died in a 1967 plane crash. The following year, "Dock of the Bay," another late-1960s masterpiece, became his biggest single. Had he lived, Redding might have become a superstar.

las, with lead singer Martha Reeves (1941–), who recorded what arguably was the one single that captured the essence of Motown: "Dancing in the Street," an all-time-great 1960s dance song.

❖ POP ART

Pop Art was the reigning art movement of the 1960s. Pop Artists offered commentary on the triteness of popular culture by incorporating mass-produced, consumer-oriented images into their paintings, sculptures, and prints: logos of commercial products, for example, or everyday objects and likenesses of celebrities. The point was that such images are so ingrained in our culture and our consciousness that they become a form of art. To make their point, artists of the decade reproduced these images as works of art, to be hung on museum or gallery walls.

Andy Warhol (1930–1987), the guru of Pop Art, earned international celebrity by duplicating images of Campbell's soup cans, Coca-Cola bottles, Brillo soap pad boxes, and stylized likenesses of such pop culture icons as Marilyn Monroe (1926–1962). Eventually, he became an avant-garde filmmaker. His early efforts avoid any responsibility for telling a story. Among the more famous were *Sleep* (1963), which depicted a man asleep for eight hours, and *Empire* (1965), a continuous nighttime image of New York's Empire State Building. Warhol eventually incorporated storylines, but his scripts were insubstantial, if not altogether improvised, and his performers

were not so much actors as an odd assortment of artists, groupies, and colorful personalities. A number became Warhol "superstars," and many were known by their purposefully tacky pseudonyms: Viva!; Candy Darling; Holly Woodlawn; Ultra Violet; Ondine; Mario Montez; and Ingrid Superstar. Warhol also was an expert self-promoter, and his declaration that, in our media and celebrity-obsessed culture, everyone will be famous for fifteen minutes has transcended his own celebrity and lived on well past his death.

Other important pop artists include Jasper Johns (1930–), who painted targets and versions of the American flag; James Rosenquist (1933–), who reproduced images from billboards; Jim Dine (1935–), who fastened such objects as tools, bedsprings, and discarded clothing to his canvases; Roy Lichtenstein (1923–1997), who painted colorful, oversized comic strip panels; Robert Rauschenberg (1925–), whose collages combined magazine photographs, newspapers, and paint; Claes Oldenburg (1929–), who produced larger-than-life sculptures of consumer products; and Wayne Thiebaud (1920–), who chose objects of food as subject matter. Some of Thiebaud's titles: "Salads, Sandwiches, and Desserts"; "Candy Apples"; and "Cupcake," mirror the essence of Pop Art.

Two other art movements that came out of the 1960s were Op Art, in which artists employed optical illusions of depth or movement, and Minimalism, in which artists spotlighted pure, flat color and hard-edged geometric designs. During the latter part of the decade, the term Minimalism also described a new movement in music. While the works of some composers were becoming increasingly complex, others were basing their creations on African and Asian music, employing simpler instrumentation that often repeated phrases and rhythms. Philip Glass (1937–) is perhaps the best-known minimalist composer.

American Theatre Wing Antoinette Perry Awards (Tony Awards)

Year	Play	Musical
1960	The Miracle Worker	Fiorello! and The Sound of Music
1961	Beckett	Bye Bye Birdie
1962	A Man for All Seasons	How to Succeed in Business Without Really Trying
1963	Who's Afraid of Virginia Woolf?	A Funny Thing Happened on the Way to the Forum
1964	Luther	Hello, Dolly!
1965	The Subject Was Roses	Fiddler on the Roof
1966	The Persecution and Assassination of Jean-Paul Marat as Performed by the Inmates of the Asylum of Charenton Under the Direction of the Marquis de Sade	Man of La Mancha
1967	The Homecoming	Cabaret
1968	Rosencrantz and Guildenstern are Dead	Hallelujah, Baby!
1969	The Great White Hope	1776

Each of these movements caused a stir in the art world. Many people complained that Pop Art, Op Art, and Minimalism required no originality or talent. The arguments about such art drew nearly as much attention as the works themselves, helping make celebrities of Warhol and others.

❖ NEW VOICES IN THEATER AND LITERATURE

The beginning of the 1960s saw a spate of successful musicals coming to Broadway, including *The Unsinkable Molly Brown; Bye Bye Birdie; How to Succeed in Business Without Really Trying; A Funny Thing Happened on the Way to the Forum; Hello, Dolly!; Funny Girl;* and *Fiddler on the Roof.* However, the stage event that defined the latter part of the decade was *Hair,* a new kind of musical. *Hair,* which came to Broadway in 1968, celebrated the era's youth culture by depicting such out-of-the-mainstream characters as sexually liberated, drug-using hippies and anti-Vietnam war

OPPOSITE PAGE
Painter Jasper Johns, who painted versions of the American flag, was a member of the Pop Art movement. Reproduced by permission of the Corbis Corporation.

Pulitzer Prizes In Fiction

Year	Title	Author
1960	*Advise and Consent*	Allen Drury
1961	*To Kill a Mockingbird*	Harper Lee
1962	*The Edge of Sadness*	Edwin O'Connor
1963	*The Rivers*	William Faulkner
1964	no award	
1965	*The Keepers of the House*	Shirley Ann Grau
1966	*The Collected Stories of Katherine Ann Porter*	Katherine Ann Porter
1967	*The Fixer*	Bernard Malamud
1968	*The Confessions of Nat Turner*	William Styron
1969	*House Made of Dawn*	N. Scott Momaday

protesters. *Hair* also was experimental in that it focused on thematic content and the depiction of a lifestyle, instead of plot and character development. Its score was rock music-inspired, and *Hair* can fairly be labeled as the original rock musical. It also became well known for a brief but controversial nude scene at the end of Act I.

Paralleling the British Invasion in music, a new generation of playwrights from the United Kingdom, including Harold Pinter (1930–) and Tom Stoppard (1937–), enjoyed success on the American stage. New American writers also emerged. Edward Albee (1928–) was perhaps the most heralded. Albee's biggest success was *Who's Afraid of Virginia Woolf?* (1962), a stark drama spotlighting the bitter conversation between two couples during one turbulent evening. Neil Simon (1927–), perhaps the most commercially successful playwright of all time, inaugurated a long-running series of light comedies during the decade.

Meanwhile, the hot new books spotlighted black humor and youthful alienation. Kurt Vonnegut Jr. (1922–) published a series of tart, cynical science fiction novels, including *Cat's Cradle* (1963), *God Bless You, Mr. Rosewater* (1965), and *Slaughterhouse Five* (1969), which were favorites on college campuses. The hero of *One Flew Over the Cuckoo's Nest* (1962), by Ken Kesey (1935–2001), was Randle J. McMurphy, a spirited mental patient who attempts to subvert an authoritarian bureaucracy. Another classic of the era was *Catch-22* (1961), by Joseph Heller (1923–1999). The novel's title rapidly became part of the American language. Heller's main character is Yossarian, a World War II bombardier who wishes to cease fighting and return home. The only trouble is, in order to do so, he must fly additional combat missions. "Catch-22" now refers to anything unreasonable or illogical. For example, you are rejected for a job because you lack experience—yet how are you to gain experience if no one will hire you? The book's antiwar/antimilitary bureaucracy tone also resonated with the young.

❖ TELEVISION STICKS TO THE TRIED AND TRUE

The 1960s mostly was a decade of business as usual for the television industry. An array of drama, comedy, adventure, sci-fi, and variety series entertained millions of viewers, with a few—including *The Dick Van Dyke Show* (1961–66), *The Andy Griffith Show* (1960–68), *The Twilight Zone* (1959–65), *Mission: Impossible* (1966–73), and *Star Trek* (1966–69)—becoming bona fide small screen classics.

Shows featuring a range of characters, from doctors (*Dr. Kildare* [1961–66], *Ben Casey* [1961–66]) to rubes (*The Beverly Hillbillies* [1962–71], *Petticoat Junction* [1963–70], *Green Acres* [1965–71]), were popular. However, if one TV series reflected the changes in American culture during the decade, it was *Rowan & Martin's Laugh-In* (1968–73), a landmark variety show that featured wacky, innovative comedy. Young people in particular adored the show for its goofy humor and sense of mischief. A host of catch phrases introduced on the show came into common usage, including "sock it to me," "here come da judge," and "you bet your sweet bippy."

In the news field, the influence of TV journalists over their print colleagues continued to grow in a trend that had begun during the previous decade. Two singular events foreshadowed the future with regard to the sheer power of television and the medium's impact on news coverage and political campaigning. The first: the televised debates between presidential

Leonard Nimoy (left) and William Shatner in a scene from Star Trek: The Motion Picture. *The television series* Star Trek *was such a big hit that it led to several successful motion pictures as well as four television spin-offs.* **Reproduced by permission of the Kobal Collection.**

candidates John F. Kennedy (1917–1963) and Richard M. Nixon (1913–1994) during the 1960 election, from which emerged the notion that voters will look favorably on a candidate based on how he looks, rather than on what he says. The second: the live coverage of events in the wake of the November 22, 1963 assassination of President John F. Kennedy, which served to unite the nation in time of grief.

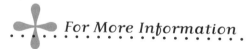

For More Information

BOOKS

Aronson, Marc. *Art Attack: A Short Cultural History of the Avant-Garde.* New York: Clarion Books, 1998.

Beck, Ken, and Jim Clark. *The Andy Griffith Show Book.* New York: St. Martin's Press, 1995.

Bergamini, Andrea. *The History of Rock Music.* Hauppauge, NY: Barron's, 2000.

Brooks, Tim. *The Complete Dictionary of Prime Time TV Stars.* New York: Ballantine Books, 1987.

Brooks, Tim, and Earle Marsh. *The Complete Directory of Prime Time Network and Cable TV Shows.* 4th ed. New York: Ballantine Books, 1999.

Calabro, Marian. *Zap!: A Brief History of Television.* New York: Maxwell Macmillan International, 1992.

Clifford, Mike, consultant. *The Illustrated History of Black Music.* New York: Harmony Books, 1982.

Epstein, Dan. *The 60's (20th Century Pop Culture).* Broomall, PA: Chelsea House, 2000.

Feinstein, Stephen. *The 1960s from the Vietnam War to Flower Power.* Berkeley Heights, NJ: Enslow, 2000.

Ford, Carin T. *Andy Warhol: Pioneer of Pop Art.* Berkeley Heights, NJ: Enslow Publishers, 2001.

Gourley, Catherine. *Media Wizards: A Behind-the-Scenes Look at Media Manipulations.* Brookfield, CT: Twenty-First Century Books, 1999.

Gourse, Leslie. *Aretha Franklin: Lady Soul.* New York: Franklin Watts, 1995.

Grant, R.G. *The Sixties.* Austin, TX: Raintree Steck-Vaughn, 2000.

Halliwell, Sarah, ed. *The 20th Century: Post-1945 Artists, Writers, and Composers.* Austin, TX: Raintree Steck-Vaughn, 1998.

Holland, Gini. *The 1960s.* San Diego, CA: Lucent Books, 1999.

Katz, Ephraim. *The Film Encyclopedia.* 4th ed. New York: HarperResource, 2001.

Knapp, Ron. *American Legends of Rock.* Springfield, NJ: Enslow Publishers, 1996.

Krafsur, Richard, exec. ed. *The American Film Institute Catalog of Motion Pictures, Feature Films, 1961–1970.* New York: R. Bowker, 1976.

Kramer, Barbara. *Ron Howard: Child Star & Hollywood Director.* Springfield, NJ: Enslow Publishers, 1998.

Maltin, Leonard, ed. *Leonard Maltin's Movie Encyclopedia.* New York: Dutton, 1994.

Maltin, Leonard, ed. *Movie & Video Guide.* 22nd ed. New York: Signet, 2001.

Martin, Marvin. *The Beatles: The Music Was Never the Same.* New York: Franklin Watts, 1996.

McNeil, Alex. *Total Television.* 4th ed. New York: Penguin Books, 1996.

Powe-Temperley, Kitty. *The 60s: Mods & Hippies.* Milwaukee, WI: Gareth Stevens, 2000.

Sheafer, Silvia Anne. *Aretha Franklin: Motown Superstar.* Springfield, NJ: Enslow Publishers, 1996.

Shirley, David. *The History of Rock & Roll.* New York: Franklin Watts, 1987.

Vaughan, William H. T. *Encyclopedia of Artists.* New York: Oxford University Press, 2000.

Waldman, Allison J. *The Barbra Streisand Scrapbook.* Secaucus, NJ: Citadel Press, 1995.

Waldron, Vince. *The Official Dick Van Dyke Show Book.* New York: Hyperion, 1994.

Wright, David K. *John Lennon: The Beatles and Beyond.* Springfield, NJ: Enslow Publishers, 1996.

WEB SITES

An American Cultural History: 1960–1969. http://www.nhmccd.edu/contracts/lrc/kc/decade60.html (accessed on August 12, 2002).

1960's Flashback—1960's Movies. http://www.1960sflashback.com/1960/Movies.asp (accessed on August 12, 2002).

1960's Flashback—TV. http://www.1960sflashback.com/1960/TV.asp (accessed on August 12, 2002).

Business and the Economy

1960: **January 4** The longest steel strike in American history, begun in July 1959, ends when the United Steel Workers union and steel companies agree on a wage increase.

1960: **May 15** The Tax Foundation reports that 25 percent of American workers' earnings are taxed.

1961: **February 23** A six-day airline strike, the costliest in history, ends.

1961: **May 5** President John F. Kennedy signs the Fair Labor Standards Act, increasing the minimum wage from $1 to $1.25 by September 1963.

1962: **January 18** New York City electrical workers negotiate a contract allowing them a twenty-five-hour workweek, plus five overtime hours.

1962: **March 1** In the largest antitrust case to date, a federal district court orders E. I. Du Pont de Nemours and Company to divest itself of 63 million shares of General Motors stock.

1962: **April 10** United States Steel announces a 3.5 percent price hike. Other major steel companies do the same, and President Kennedy denounces the action.

1962: **May 28** In the single greatest daily loss since 1929, the New York Stock Exchange plummets by nearly $21 billion. Fortunately, stocks quickly rebound.

1962: **July 27** A price-fixing scandal ends with General Electric consenting to pay $7.5 million in damages for earning excessive profits.

1962: **September 15** To stimulate projects in economically depressed regions, President Kennedy signs into law a $900 million public works bill.

1962: **October 4** To increase overseas trade through tariff reductions (tariffs are taxes on imported and exported goods), the U.S. Congress passes the Trade Expansion Act.

1963: **January 26** A nearly month-long longshoremen's strike ends. The shipping industry loses more than $800 million.

1963: **March 31** A 114-day New York City newspaper strike ends, costing publishers $100 million.

1964: **February 26** The Tax Reduction Act lowers personal and corporate income tax rates.

1964: **September 25** The United Auto Workers strike at General Motors. A contract agreement is reached two weeks later, but local strikers hinder production for another month.

1965: **December 5** In order to control inflation, the Federal Reserve Board raises the discount rate from 4 to 4.5 percent, the highest rate in 45 years.

1966: **March 22** The president of General Motors publicly apologizes to consumer advocate Ralph Nader for spying on Nader's private life.

1966: **April 6** The United Farm Workers, which for seven months had been striking against California grape growers, proclaims victory when it becomes the official bargaining agent for Schenley Industries' farm workers.

1966: **September 9** President Lyndon Johnson signs into law the Traffic Safety Act, establishing safety standards for automobiles.

1966: **October 7** In the worst decline since 1962, the Dow Jones industrial average plummets to 744 points.

1967: **July 5** The Federal Communications Commission orders American Telephone and Telegraph (AT&T) to reduce its yearly overseas and long-distance rates by $120 million.

1967: **July 26** A three-month-long United Rubber Workers strike ends with the union signing a three-year contract with tire manufacturers. Five days later, Firestone announces price increases.

1968: **January 15** The Supreme Court approves a New York Central and Pennsylvania railroads merger, creating the country's largest railroad.

1968: **February 19** The first statewide teachers' strike in American history begins in Florida. The walkout of nearly half the state's teachers ends on March 8.

1968: **April 18** For the first time, Bell Telephone System workers walk off the job. A settlement is announced in May.

1968: **June 13** The New York Stock Exchange sets a record with 2.35 million shares exchanged in one day.

1968: **July 30** Eleven major steel companies reach a three-year agreement with the United Steel Workers of America.

1969: **February 26** General Motors recalls 4.9 million potentially defective cars and trucks.

1969: **July 23** Consumer prices increase 6.4 percent since January, the largest rise since 1951.

Overview

The American economy flourished during the 1960s, as it had during the previous decade. Despite dips at various points throughout the decade, the Dow Jones Industrial Average, a composite of the prices of thirty top U.S. industrial stocks, and the figure most often quoted when evaluating stock market activity, steadily rose. In January 1966, it topped 1,000 for the first time. Increasing numbers of Americans owned stock and, between 1962 and 1968, stock market growth outdistanced the booming market (or bull market) of the 1920s. Inflation (an increase in currency circulating in the economy, leading to a sharp decrease in its value and a rise in prices) and recession (a temporary decrease in business activity at a time when it had been thriving) were familiar words to business and economy watchers during the 1960s, and in decades to come. However, unlike the 1920s, the 1960s stock market boom was not followed by a depression (an extended period characterized by decreased business activity, increased joblessness, and falling wages and prices).

Despite this prosperity, major shifts were occurring in American business and the workforce. Preexisting corporations were merging and becoming larger, more powerful conglomerates. Consumers increasingly were doing their shopping at discount chain stores and their dining at inexpensive fast-food restaurants, leading to a decrease in the number of single-proprietor businesses. Small farms, and a cherished American way of life, were becoming extinct. Larger, often corporate-owned, farms were replacing family farms, and newly developed farm technology was increasing farm output. Meanwhile, manufacturers were relocating from the Northeast and Midwest to nonunion Southern states, taking jobs with them and robbing industrial cities of their vitality. Manufacturers also were opening factories in foreign countries to take further advantage of cheap labor. These shifts led to a decline in the power of unions.

America was becoming less reliant on industrial and manufacturing industries, as the rapid development of high-tech electronics led to the dawn of the Information Age. Now more than ever, workers found themselves sitting at desks and pushing papers, rather than tilling the soil, working on assembly lines, or making products with their hands. Adding to all this was the increasing presence of women in the workforce. Some took jobs for practical purposes, such as to add to the family income. Young women, in particular, were also being affected by the growing feminist movement. They wanted the freedom to choose their own lifestyles, to pursue professional careers, and to have alternatives to being full-time homemakers.

The automobile boom of the 1950s continued into the 1960s. However, car buyers increasingly chose smaller, less-expensive, more energy-efficient cars. Many of these were produced by foreign automakers. The Detroit automakers soon developed their own lines of smaller, sportier cars.

During the 1960s, big business increasingly offered financial support to the arts. Museums and performing arts organizations were unable to meet rising expenses solely on the basis of ticket sales or admission fees. Corporate America increasingly funded arts organizations, resulting in waves of publicity and goodwill for big business.

In 1965, President Lyndon Johnson declared that he envisioned the United States evolving into a "Great Society," a nation of abundance, in which poverty and blight would be eradicated. In such a nation, all American workers would have jobs, and all would be sufficiently paid. However, the events of the decade, and of those to come, derailed plans for Johnson's "Great Society."

Mary Kay Ash (c.1915–2001) A divorceé and mother of three, Mary Kay Ash entered the workforce out of necessity. A sales position with Stanley Home Products, in which she demonstrated the company's merchandise in people's homes, started her off on a career that culminated in her establishing her own company, Beauty by Mary Kay (soon changed to Mary Kay Cosmetics), in 1963. Her "beauty consultants" organized house parties for women, where they offered beauty tips and make-up lessons and sold a line of Mary Kay cosmetics. Sales rose from $198,000 in 1964 to $800,000 the following year. By 1968, annual sales had topped $10 million. *Photo reproduced by permission of Mary Kay Inc.*

Cesar Chavez (1927–1993) Cesar Chavez first became a political organizer during the 1950s by arranging nonviolent marches and economic boycotts to focus national attention on the plight of Mexican American migrant workers. He was general director of the Community Service Organization (CSO), a California-based self-help social service group. When CSO rejected his idea of organizing farm workers into a union, Chavez bolted and created the United Farm Workers Association, which later merged with an AFL-CIO affiliate, becoming what eventually was known as the United Farm Workers of America (UFW). *Photo reproduced by permission of AP/Wide World Photos.*

James Ling (1922–) James Ling founded Ling-Temco-Vought (LTV), one of the 1960s most diversified conglomerates. Just after World War II, he established the Ling Electric Company, which specialized in residential electrical wiring. He expanded the company throughout the 1950s by acquiring other companies, including Temco Electronics, an electronic-reconnaissance equipment manufacturer, and Chance Vought, a producer of aircraft. All these holdings were united, resulting in LTV. In 1965, *Fortune* magazine dubbed LTV the fastest-expanding company in the United States. However, two decades later, in the wake of a downward-spiraling economy and heavy debt load, LTV filed for bankruptcy. *Photo reproduced by permission of the Corbis Corporation.*

Ralph Nader (1934–) Over the decades, Ralph Nader and his staff of "Nader's Raiders" have been America's leading consumer advocates. Nader first gained the national spotlight in 1965 with his best-selling book, *Unsafe at Any Speed,* in which he criticized General Motors for marketing a car, the Chevrolet Corvair, which had acknowledged safety defects. In the 2000 presidential election, Nader ran on the Green Party ticket. His refusal to exit the race, despite the certainty of his defeat, is believed to have cost Democrat Al Gore (1948–) the crucial votes he needed to defeat Republican George W. Bush (1946–). *Photo reproduced courtesy of the Library of Congress.*

H. Ross Perot (1930–) H. Ross Perot first carved out a career as a successful business entrepreneur. A former top salesman at IBM, he established Electronic Data Systems (EDS), a computer-service company, in 1962. Six years later, he took the firm public (offered shares of company stock for sale) and emerged a billionaire. Perot later became the largest stockholder in General Motors and a member of its board of directors. He also made headlines in the late-1960s for his unsuccessful efforts to rescue American prisoners-of-war from Vietnam. *Photo reproduced by permission of the Corbis Corporation.*

An Wang (1920–1990) In 1948, An Wang received a Ph.D. in applied physics from Harvard. He correctly foresaw the growth potential inherent in the then-infant computer industry and, in 1951, founded his own firm, Wang Laboratories. In the 1950s and 1960s and beyond, Wang Laboratories was at the cutting edge of electronics technology. Among its more popular innovations was the first electronic sports stadium scoreboard, installed at Shea Stadium in New York. Wang also personally held more than thirty-five patents relating to computer technology.

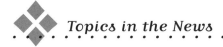

❖ FARMING IN AMERICA

The nation's slow but steady change from an agrarian (farm-based) to an industrial society, and the relocation of millions from the farm to the city, was a reality of American life through much of the twentieth-century. The 1960s saw the continued evolution of rural America and the further erosion of traditional American farm life.

During the decade, 900,000 small farms disappeared. Many were consolidated into larger concerns or were swallowed up by preexisting companies. As a result, the average farm size increased from 297 acres in 1960 to 374 acres ten years later. Despite the problems of the individual farmer, breakthroughs in farm technology, including state-of-the-art machinery and new pesticides and fertilizers along with the introduction of assembly line techniques into agriculture, helped raise the value of farm output from $29 billion in 1946 to $54 billion in 1970. Chickens no longer freely roamed the farm, gobbling up whatever edibles happened to be in their path. They now were housed in controlled environments and fed special foods that would quickly fatten them up for market.

Meanwhile, the partnership between the farmer and the federal government forged during the Depression continued. Farm owners benefited from government price supports, loans, and subsidies; occasionally, in order to uphold agricultural prices, farmers were paid not to cultivate their lands. Such payments rose from $702 million in 1960 to $3.7 billion in 1970.

❖ SMALLER CARS FROM FOREIGN LANDS

The prosperity of the 1960s allowed America to continue its love affair with automobiles. In fact, two cars per family—one for him and one for her—became a status symbol among the widening middle class. In 1960, three major American manufacturers dominated the automobile industry: General Motors, Ford, and Chrysler. At the dawn of the decade, this trio accounted for a whopping 93 percent of all cars sold in the United States, and a respectable 48 percent of global sales.

However, during the previous decade, smaller imported cars, produced by such companies as Volkswagen, Fiat, Renault, Toyota, and Datsun, began to appear on American highways. The inexpensive, easy-to-repair Volkswagen Beetle proved especially popular, particularly among the young. In 1968, Volkswagen accounted for 68 percent of all foreign car sales in the United States.

To meet the competition, Detroit automakers began producing small cars of their own—the Corvair (General Motors), Falcon (Ford), and Valiant (Chrysler)—along with sleek sports cars like the Ford Mustang. For a while in mid-decade, it appeared that the Big Three had beaten back the competition, with import sales dropping from 668,000 to 540,000 between 1959 and 1965. However, by decade's end, the foreign companies—and, in particular, Volkswagen, Toyota, and Datsun—were once again threatening American automakers. The imports were aided first by a recession, and then by two oil crises during the following decade, which made buyers want cars that were smaller and more fuel-efficient. At the close of the 1960s, 11 percent of all cars purchased in the United States were imports. By 1987, that number had risen to 31 percent.

❖ BIG BUSINESS, THE ARTS, AND PUBLIC BROADCASTING

During the 1960s, big business and the arts became increasingly linked. In order to meet rising expenses, museums, theater companies, and dance troupes turned to corporate sponsorship. In 1962, S. S. Johnson and Son (of Johnson's Wax) paid $750,000 for 102 works by contemporary American painters. The following year, American Export and Isbrandtsen Lines gave the New York Metropolitan Opera $135,000 to stage a production of *Aida,* by Giuseppe Verdi (1813–1901). In 1967, the Ford Foundation funded the *Public Television Laboratory,* an innovative, two-hour-long news and features program that aired on educational television. In fact, between 1951 and 1977, the Ford Foundation donated almost $300 million to public television and radio.

With the passage of the Public Broadcasting Act of 1967, the federal government became involved in funneling money to educational television stations and underwriting noncommercial programming. However, such programming still depended upon financial support from organizations like the Ford Foundation and corporate sponsors.

All parties benefited from such arrangements. Individual artists and their affiliated organizations secured the funds that allowed them to continue their endeavors; viewers benefited from the availability of increased cultural and education-oriented programming; and corporations earned free publicity and the goodwill of artists and arts patrons.

❖ BOOM ON WALL STREET

In 1949, the Dow Jones Industrial Average, a composite of the prices of thirty top U.S. industrial stocks, and the figure most often quoted when evaluating stock market activity, stood at 161. It rose steadily during the

From 1962 through 1968, the New York Stock Exchange experienced its greatest increase since the economic boom years of the 1920s. Reproduced by permission of the Corbis Corporation.

following decade, topping out at 685 in 1959. Then in the early 1960s, the Dow flattened. In 1962, it endured its worst year since 1931, which had been the height of the Great Depression. By June of that year, its value had declined by 27 percent over the previous six months.

Happily, the future of the Dow was rosy. From mid-1962 through 1966, it shot up 460 points. In January 1966, the Dow even rose above 1,000. All told, the market increase from 1962 through 1968 was even greater than during the economic boom years of the 1920s.

During the decade, almost thirty million Americans owned stocks. Despite this, few understood the inner workings of the market, preferring to invest in mutual funds (diversified investment funds, managed by professionals, whose shares can be bought and sold at any time, at a price that reflects their total value). In 1965, one-quarter of all New York Stock Exchange transactions involved mutual funds. Three years later, financial concerns were introducing new mutual funds at the rate of one-per-week. Fund managers were controlling assets worth more than $51 billion.

One of the more noteworthy mutual funds was the Fidelity Capital Fund, which started in 1957. Unlike the more traditional mutual funds, which invested in a range of stocks, Fidelity concentrated on the emerging technology-oriented companies, among them Polaroid, Litton, Xerox, and Texas Instruments. It quickly became one of the fastest-growing mutual funds. After some difficult times during the 1962 stock market crisis, the Fidelity Capital Fund became one of the most successful measures of a strong economy.

❖ CHAIN STORES AND FRANCHISES

During the nineteenth century, small, single-proprietor businesses, otherwise known as "mom-and-pop" enterprises, competed with each other for the consumer dollar. Consumers could choose from a limited range of goods in a "general store," which stocked food, clothing, appliances, and basic household items. There were also shops that specialized in such products as hardware and tools, toys, or men's and women's clothing. Food was purchased from shopkeepers who made their living by focusing on one type of food: meat products were sold directly to consumers in butcher shops and bakers created breads, cookies, and cakes and sold them in bakeries.

In the twentieth century, larger all-purpose stores began to take the place of these smaller, more individualized shops. Single-store owners had difficulty competing with supermarket chains, which stocked their shelves with a variety of foods all in one store, and department stores, which sold many types of merchandise, allowing customers a convenient, one-stop-shopping experience.

The 1960s gave birth to yet another retail revolution: the arrival of the all-purpose discount chain store. These featured the same array of products found elsewhere. However, prices usually were lower because the chain stores purchased goods in bulk, enabling them to under-price the competition while still maintaining profitability.

The first discount retailer was Kmart, which debuted in 1962 in Garden City, Michigan, a Detroit suburb. By 1970, more than four hundred Kmarts were in operation across the United States; in future decades, that number would expand into the thousands. Other successful discount chains included Wal-Mart and Target, which also began business in 1962, but Kmart was the first to open stores across the United States.

Meanwhile, franchises such as McDonald's and Holiday Inn began sprouting up across the country. For the individual entrepreneur, franchising combined the benefits of small and large businesses. Franchise holders

Kmart was one of many large, discount, all-purpose stores that debuted during the 1960s. Reproduced by permission of Hulton Archive.

Trading Stamps

Trading stamps, which were collected by patrons who purchased goods and services and placed in blank books that were filled and redeemed for prizes, had been in existence since the 1890s. But it was during the 1960s that they soared in popularity. Trading stamp companies such as Sperry and Hutchinson (S&H Green Stamps) sold their stamps to retailers, who used them to induce customer purchases. Patrons eventually traded the stamps for a range of items, including furniture, sheets, blankets, appliances, and sporting goods.

In 1966, more than three hundred trading stamp companies were in business across the nation, and it was reported that 83 percent of all American households collected the stamps.

worked for themselves, operating a legally independent business, yet they were offering "name-brand" goods or services. Often, the parent company trained them. At McDonald's, new franchise holders attended "Hamburger University" to learn to operate the business to McDonald's standards. They also benefited from Madison Avenue advertising campaigns designed and paid for by the national office. Indeed, "McDonald's" and "Holiday Inn" were brand names as well as locations that customers chose for a particular and predictable outcome. Consumers choosing to dine at a McDonald's or spend a night at a Holiday Inn did so expecting a certain consistency in the product or service they were purchasing, not to mention value for their dollar.

By 1967, sales from franchises accounted for 10 percent of the nation's Gross National Product (GNP; a measure of the total value of goods and services produced by a nation during a year). Just as had happened earlier with general stores and butcher shops, the steady increase in such franchises as McDonald's and Holiday Inn led to a decline in the number of nonfranchised, family-owned hamburger parlors and roadside motels, while the popularity of such ice cream franchises as Baskin-Robbins and Dairy Queen led to the demise of the corner ice cream parlor. Eventually, the goods and services offered by franchises came to include everything from car repair (Midas Muffler) to moving equipment rental (U-Haul) to tax preparation (H & R Block).

❖ DOW CHEMICAL AND STUDENT ACTIVISTS

During the 1960s, peace activists and civil rights advocates used the forum of public protest to express their views to the powers-that-be and win publicity for their cause. As the war in Vietnam escalated from mid-decade on, increasing numbers of college students became actively involved in marching against the war. At the time, Dow Chemical had secured a government contract to produce napalm, a gasoline gel which was packed in canisters and dropped by bombers on the Vietnam countryside. Napalm was devised to stick to the skin and burn those who came in contact with it. For this reason, it, and Dow Chemical, became a symbol of the inhumanity of war in general and U.S. foreign policy in Vietnam in particular.

On May 28, 1966, one hundred demonstrators paraded outside a Dow Chemical plant in Torrance, California. Meanwhile, seventy-five protesters lined up in front of the company's New York office and chanted, "Napalm burns babies. Dow makes money." However, not all anti-Dow protests were peaceful. The following year, student activists harassed a Dow employment recruiter at the University of Wisconsin-Madison. The resulting scuffle left sixty-five students and seven police personnel hospitalized. At other times, company offices were vandalized and records were destroyed.

At first, Dow justified its napalm production by stating, "Our position on the manufacture of napalm is that we are a supplier of goods to the Defense Department and not a policymaker. We do not and should not try to decide military strategy or policy." Yet public protests and an increasing awareness of the potency and purpose of napalm resulted in a negative public image for the company. Dow elected not to aggressively pursue its government contract for napalm production when it came up for renewal. The company eventually lost the contract to a lower bidder.

❖ HIGH-TECH ELECTRONICS

The 1960s was the dawn of the Information Age. Spearheading this evolution was the development of high-tech electronics. Wang Laboratories, founded by electronics and computer industry pioneer An Wang (1920–1990), became a high-tech giant. In 1955, Wang patented the magnetic "Pulse Transfer Controlling Device," which regulated the flow of magnetic energy. A decade later, he introduced "LOCI," the initial desktop computer that generated logarithms (the exponent of the power to which a fixed number must be raised in order to produce a given number) with a single keystroke. Wang later incorporated this technology into the creation of the electronic desk calculator. In the 1970s and 1980s, Wang became a leading producer of word processors and desktop computers, which then primarily were used in laboratories, businesses, and schools.

Despite Wang's innovations, the corporate name most often identified with the computer industry was IBM (International Business Machines). The company's president, Thomas J. Watson Jr. (1914–1993), like An Wang, sensed the potential of computer technology as an essential business tool. By the mid-1960s, IBM so dominated the computer business that critics often referred to the industry's top manufacturers as "IBM and the Seven Dwarfs." In 1965, IBM controlled a whopping 65.3 percent of the market computer manufacturing market. Sperry Rand came in a distant second, at 12.1 percent. The five corporations that followed all had single-digit percentages: Control Data (5.4); Honeywell (3.8); Burroughs (3.5); General Electric (3.4); RCA (2.9); and NCR (2.9).

❖ KENNEDY VERSUS BIG STEEL

One of the early major domestic crises faced by President John F. Kennedy (1917–1963) after his inauguration in 1961 involved the American steel industry. Labor negotiations between the industry and its workers had been ongoing. The president intervened in the hope of keeping industry costs down, and in March 1962 a deal was reached whereby steelworkers would receive added fringe benefits but no salary increase. Kennedy believed that, with the settlement agreed upon, the industry would not raise prices. Yet almost immediately, U.S. Steel proclaimed that it would hike prices by 3.5 percent ($6 per ton). Other major steel companies did the same, and the president believed he had been deceived. He denounced the increases in a televised speech and initiated a grand jury investigation into industry price-fixing. Congress hinted that it too might inquire into industry business practices, while the Pentagon, an important steel industry customer, threatened to purchase the material only from companies that had not raised prices. Three days after the hikes were reported, several steel firms cancelled them. U.S. Steel soon followed suit.

While the steel-industry crisis had been averted, its aftereffects lingered and damaged relations between big business and the Democratic Party. Upon entering office, Kennedy had determined to work to obliterate American industry's long-standing apprehension of the party. However, this incident only further convinced the private sector that Kennedy and the Democrats were antibig business.

❖ LABOR AND THE "GREAT SOCIETY"

Through the mid-1960s, in a carryover from the previous decade, American workers kept realizing their American dreams. Union member-

ship was holding steady or increasing and so were wages. Labor-friendly
Democrats were in the White House: John F. Kennedy (1917–1963) ended
eight years of Republican control of the government's executive branch
when he was elected president in 1960, and Lyndon Johnson (1908–1973),

who took office upon Kennedy's assassination, won reelection in 1964. Johnson's ambitious plans for a "Great Society," first revealed in a 1964 speech at the University of Michigan commencement ceremony, certainly pleased the American worker. Johnson's aim was to fashion a nation that offered "abundance and liberty for all," not to mention an "end to poverty and racial injustice." Liberal Democrats lauded Johnson's vision, which included such social reform concepts as health care for the lower classes, medical care for the aged, federal support for education, and legal refuge for blacks deprived of their right to vote because of state regulations. It was the most extensive proposal for social-oriented federal legislation since the New Deal of President Franklin Roosevelt (1882–1945) during the 1930s.

However, as the decade wore on, it became obvious that the power of American labor was in decline. For one thing, more manufacturers were relocating their plants either away from the Northeast or Midwest to the South, where many states were not union-friendly, or to foreign countries, where workers could be paid salaries fractions of those expected by American workers. Between 1966 and 1976, northeastern states lost one million manufacturing jobs, while 860,000 became available down south; by the early 1970s, more than one-third of the labor force employed by such major American corporations as Ford, Kodak, International Telephone and Telegraph (ITT), and Procter and Gamble was foreign-based. The AFL-CIO (American Federation of Labor-Congress of Industrial Organizations, an umbrella association of unions) calculated that, between 1966 and 1971, foreign branches of American firms were employing one million additional workers. All of this resulted in the mass closings of northern manufacturing plants. Once-bustling industrial cities, mill towns, and manufacturing centers became ghost towns, where poverty and unemployment reigned.

The bottom line was that there were fewer higher-paying industrial jobs available for unskilled American workers. The dawn of the Information Age did create millions of service-oriented positions that did not require skills or education. However, these jobs, many of which were clerical in nature, or involved fast-food preparation, did not pay as well as the manufacturing and industrial jobs had paid. By 1970, jobs for blue-collar workers had declined to the point where they were outnumbered by white-collar positions. One AFL-CIO official lamented that the United States was evolving into "a country stripped of industrial capacity and meaningful work…a service economy…a nation of citizens busily buying and selling cheeseburgers and root beer floats."

The public-sector union movement was negatively affected by these job shifts and was further eroded by the era's social upheaval. Many American union leaders supported the war in Vietnam and were slow to back

OPPOSITE PAGE
Cesar Chavez and the United Farm Workers organized and participated in a successful grape strike, in which grape pickers in California fought for higher wages and better working conditions.
Reproduced by permission of Magnum Photos, Inc.

What Things Cost

In the early 1960s, New Yorkers paid $.15 to ride a subway or bus. A slice of pizza cost $.15 or $.20, while a tuna fish sandwich would set you back between $.45 and $.65. The price of a ticket to a first-run feature in an upscale Manhattan movie house was between $2 and $2.50. At a "five-and-dime store" such as Woolworth's, a consumer could still find scores of items that actually cost five or ten cents.

In 1967, the average price nationally for a three-bedroom house was $17,000. A new Cadillac cost $6,700, while the latest Volkswagen cost $1,497. Regular gas was $.39 per gallon. The purchase of a gray flannel suit cost a man $60. A portable typewriter (this was nearly two decades before the age of the personal computer) cost $39, while a pound of sirloin steak was $.89, and a Hershey chocolate bar cost a whopping $.5!

the efforts of African Americans to gain their civil rights. These developments resulted in a generation of young Americans coming to perceive unions and their leaders as reactionary. At one time, union activists were acknowledged to be battlers against those in power for the rights of workers. Now, those very same labor leaders were viewed as having secret partnerships with corporate America.

❖ THE RISE OF CONGLOMERATES

Along with the decline of the blue-collar American workforce and the power of the unions that represented them came a rapid rise in corporate expansion and an increase in company mergers. Unlike other periods in American history in which mergers were dominant, for the first time companies that offered unrelated products or services began linking. They chose this corporate strategy figuring that the resulting diversification would protect them from economic downturns in specific industries.

One example of how this strategy was implemented is the manner in which International Telephone and Telegraph (ITT) diversified its holdings. ITT originally was a telecommunications company that operated in foreign countries. Between 1961 and 1968, ITT purchased 52 companies with total assets of $1.5 billion. Among them: Avis (rental cars); Conti-

In 1936, a Gallup poll reported that 18 percent of Americans approved of married women working outside the home. By the end of the 1970s, that figure had risen to 68 percent.

In 1950, approximately three of every ten American workers were women. However, many were young and single, and would quit their jobs upon marrying. By 1980, that figure had risen to over four of every ten workers. Many of these were more educated, were business and career-oriented, and were determined to balance their professional and personal lives.

nental Baking (bread and cake producers); Canteen Corporation (food sales); Levitt and Sons (home builders); Sheraton Corporation (hotels), and Hartford Fire Insurance. By 1974, only 20 percent of ITT's revenues came from its telecommunications division.

Tobacco companies in particular began purchasing nontobacco-related concerns. During the decade, the industry began to be threatened by increasing publicity surrounding medical research determining that smoking was a serious health hazard. Fearing a decrease in product sales, the tobacco giants diversified their holdings. American Tobacco bought Jim Beam, Master Lock, Franklin Life Insurance, and Sunshine Biscuits, and in 1969 changed its name to American Brands. The R.J. Reynolds tobacco company purchased American Independent Oil and several food producers (Chun King, Del Monte, and Morton Foods). P. Lorillard became part of the Loews motion picture theater chain. Liggett and Myers acquired Alpo dog food and Izmira vodka. The Philip Morris company purchased Seven-Up and the Miller Brewing Company.

Corporate expansion began to decline in the decade's final years, because the Justice Department began scrutinizing corporate takeovers and company profits generally were not as high as expected. A recession during the early 1970s ended the wave of mergers, which did not start up again until the 1980s.

❖ WOMEN AND WORK

Before the 1960s, the male was the traditional family breadwinner. The husband/father rose every weekday morning and went off to work, whether in an office or a factory, while the wife/mother remained at home where she cleaned the house, cooked the meals, and raised the children. However, during this decade, an ever-increasing number of older, married women entered the workforce. In certain cases, for example, as jobs in northern cities became more scarce, a second income was needed to pay the monthly bills. Among younger and more educated women, a desire to work was directly related to the growing feminist movement and the craving for professional careers and economic independence.

The increasing presence of women in the workforce did not deter the amount of sexism they encountered. Often, women only could find part-time jobs, and at salaries well below those paid to men who did comparable work. Many professions still were male-dominated; there were few women lawyers, for example, or doctors, business managers, or entrepreneurs. A woman journalist might be limited to working on what then was known as the "Woman's Page," writing about fashion or recipes, instead of covering politics, business, or sports. Before founding her own cosmetics company in 1963, Mary Kay Ash (c.1915–2001) spent a quarter-century working in sales. During this time, she experienced sexism first-hand. Ash's rationale for forming what came to be known as Mary Kay Cosmetics, she explained, was that she "just couldn't believe that a woman's brain was worth only 50 cents on the dollar."

During the 1960s, a high school girl who was the brightest in her class still was expected to attend college primarily to meet and marry her male counterpart. Among the careers open to her were teacher, nurse, or librarian. These jobs generally were lower-paid and could be left when the woman became pregnant and returned to when her children were grown.

As feminism took hold in American society in the 1970s and 1980s, a gap grew between two opposing forces: those who insisted the proper place for women was in the home rearing children, and those who believed women deserved the very same professional opportunities as men.

 For More Information

BOOKS

Celsi, Teresa Noel. *Ralph Nader: The Consumer Revolution.* Brookfield, CT: Millbrook Press, 1991.

Gay, Kathlyn. *Who's Running the Nation? How Corporate Power Threatens Democracy.* New York: Franklin Watts, 1998.

Gonzales, Doreen. *Cesar Chavez: Leader for Migrant Farm Workers.* Springfield, NJ: Enslow Publishers, 1996.

Holmes, Burnham. *Cesar Chavez: Farm Worker Activist*. Austin, TX: Raintree Steck-Vaughn, 1994.

Horwitz, Elinor Lander. *On the Land: American Agriculture from Past to Present*. New York: Atheneum, 1980.

Kroc, Ray, with Robert Anderson. *Grinding It Out: The Making of McDonald's*. Chicago: H. Regnery, 1977.

Love, John F. *McDonald's: Behind the Arches*. New York: Bantam Books, 1986.

O'Connell, Arthur J. *American Business in the 20th Century*. San Mateo, CA: Bluewood Books, 1999.

Soto, Gary. *Jessie De La Cruz: A Profile of a United Farm Worker*. New York: Persea Books, 2000.

WEB SITES

British Sports Cars vs. American Sports Cars During the 1960s and 1970s. http://www.geocities.com/pattonr1_04011/Sportscars.html (accessed on August 6, 2002).

1960s Flashback—Economy/Prices. http://www.1960sflashback.com/1960/Economy.asp (accessed on August 6, 2002).

chapter three *Education*

1960: **November 13** A special session of the Louisiana state legislature approves extreme measures to avert New Orleans school desegregation.

1960: **December 4** Ignoring ongoing abuse, a black New Orleans minister continues escorting his five-year-old daughter to an integrated school.

1961: **January 10** Two black students register at the University of Georgia. Subsequent riots lead to their suspension; however, school administrators are ordered to reinstate them.

1961: **March 20** Louisiana's efforts to stop integration are judged to be unconstitutional.

1962: **January 11** In his State of the Union address, President John F. Kennedy pledges to work to pass education-funding legislation.

1962: **February 6** President Kennedy presents his "Special Message on Education" to Congress, in which he proposes financial aid for handicapped children and illiterate adults and funding to upgrade teacher quality.

1962: **April** Years of classroom overcrowding and low pay result in a one-day strike by New York City teachers.

1962: **June 25** The U.S. Supreme Court rules unconstitutional a prayer reading in New York public schools.

1962: **July 8** The federal government announced it will initiate a study of the effect of television on schoolchildren.

1962: **July 26** A federal judge orders schools in Prince Edward County, Virginia, to reopen, three years after they were closed in defiance of integration.

1962: **August 31** Due to threats of violence, Roman Catholic Church officials close an integrated parochial school in Buras, Mississippi.

1962: **September 20** In defiance of a federal court order, James Meredith, a black man, is denied admission to the University of Mississippi.

1962: **September 30–October 1** James Meredith is escorted onto the "Ole Miss" campus. After fifteen hours of shooting and rioting in which two persons are killed, Meredith is enrolled.

1963: **January 28** Harvey Gantt becomes the first black student at South Carolina's Clemson College.

1963: **June 11** After threatening to defy a federal desegregation mandate, Governor George Wallace allows two black students to enroll at the University of Alabama.

1963: **August 11** One of the two black students at the University of Alabama drops out.

1963: **August 18** James Meredith becomes the first black Bachelor's degree candidate at the University of Mississippi.

1963: **September 8** The United Federation of Teachers agrees to a new contract, preventing a New York teachers strike.

1963: **December 16** President Lyndon Johnson signs into law the Higher Education Facilities Act of 1963.

1964: **January 8** In his State of the Union address, President Johnson asks Congress to approve additional money for education.

1964: **March 12** Thousands of New Yorkers march on the city's Board of Education to protest the elimination of neighborhood schools resulting from desegregation plans.

1964: **September–December** University of California, Berkeley students demonstrate against a ban on on-campus free speech. The protest culminates in a student strike.

1965: **March 5** The Freedom School, an integrated school in Indianola, Mississippi, is burned to the ground.

1965: **April 9** The U.S. Senate passes a $1.3 billion school-aid bill.

1965: **November 20** City University of New York (CUNY) administrators quit in protest over a new $400 tuition fee for city residents.

1966: **March 3** President Johnson signs into law the Veteran's Readjustment Act, allowing education benefits for those who served in the military after January 31, 1955.

1966: **October 20** Congress approves a $6.2 billion aid to education package.

1967: **June 30** A task force appointed by President Johnson recommends that additional federal monies be spent on education programs.

1968: **May–June** Student demonstrators at Columbia University, protesting racism and the Vietnam war, occupy several campus buildings.

1968: **November 18** The United Federation of Teachers votes to end a five-week-long New York teachers' strike.

1969: **May 7** Seven are injured in a confrontation between black and white students at New York's City College.

 *Overview*

A revolution in education took place in the United States during the 1960s. The federal government became increasingly education-oriented. Presidents John F. Kennedy and Lyndon Johnson lobbied Congress for increased federal aid to education, leading to the creation of new programs. Their efforts displeased conservative politicians and community leaders, particularly those who opposed school integration and who believed that education policy was strictly a local issue. Education policy became a hotly debated topic during the decade for two primary reasons. First, it was closely related to one of the decade's prime social movements: the fight for equal rights for black Americans. One of the key issues related to that movement was the further desegregation of America's schools, as called for by the 1954 *Brown v. Board of Education of Topeka, Kansas* Supreme Court decision. Secondly, the government refused to offer funds to private and parochial schools; this incited heated debate throughout the decade.

During the 1960s, students from grade school through university-level began studying old subjects in new ways. One of the offshoots of the civil rights movement was a change in the approach to teaching American history. Courses exploring the founding of the United States began emphasizing diversity. The struggles of black Americans for equality were added to course material, as were the experiences of Native Americans. Education theorists insisted that teachers be empowered to develop their students' minds and encourage their intellectual curiosity, rather than merely stressing learning by rote (a method of memorization). New scholastic disciplines also became available, from courses in social science, sociology, and theater arts to increasing numbers of foreign language classes. Meanwhile, bilingual education programs increased as immigrants began to insist on maintaining their native cultures and continuing to speak their native languages while simultaneously learning English.

Despite these changes, some scholars and theorists still voiced criticism of the manner in which Americans were educated. Formal schooling did little to encourage creativity or individuality, they noted. They charged that students were merely being prepared to enter the workforce and accept authority and mediocrity passively, rather than to think for themselves.

Beginning in mid-decade, young American males not only faced the draft, which was a system by which young men were called to mandatory service in the U.S. military, but also the escalation of the fighting in Vietnam. Many who might not otherwise have planned to attend college, or who might have put off continuing their education, enrolled in college straight out of high school, or applied to graduate school as soon as they achieved an undergraduate degree. As the war continued, it was fought more and more by the "under-classes": those who could not afford college tuition fees. One consequence was that military personnel, particularly the youngest members, were increasingly under-educated. To alleviate this problem, the military committed millions of dollars to fund education programs for its manpower.

Meanwhile, the struggle for civil rights and the growing unpopularity of the conflict in Vietnam led to increasing unrest and protest on university campuses. Student protests and demonstrations during the decade began with the 1964 "free speech" movement, on the campus of the University of California, Berkeley. Within a few years, thousands of students from universities large and small were actively demonstrating on campus. Their causes included the war in Vietnam, racism in American society, course content, and what they considered to be the inappropriate union between college administrators and the military-industrial complex. Often, student demonstrators were dispersed with firm police crowd-control methods.

As students petitioned and demonstrated to change the world, they also changed the rules and regulations on campuses. Student protests led to the demise of many long-standing campus regulations. Increasingly, women were no longer required to sign in and out of dormitories, or adhere to curfews. Male and female undergraduates were allowed to visit each other's dorm rooms. The formality of many college classrooms gave way to the informality of "rap sessions" and open discussion among students and teachers.

Jerome Bruner (1915–) In the late 1950s and early 1960s, Jerome Bruner, founder and codirector of the Center for Cognitive Studies at Harvard, was involved in the study of how people learn. He and his colleagues explored perception, memory, and thinking, and how they interact during the learning process. Bruner's conclusion: "Any subject can be taught effectively in some intellectually honest form to any child at any stage of development, providing attention is paid to the psychological development of the child." In other words, if teachers logically organize their teaching material with student developmental level in mind, all students can understand the true essence of a subject. *Photo courtesy of the Archives of the History of American Psychology.*

James B. Conant (1893–1978) During the 1960s James B. Conant researched and wrote about all aspects of the American educational system. He authored two books during the decade, *Slums and the Suburbs* (1961) and *Shaping Educational Policy* (1964). In these books he called for comprehensive high schools that would meet all students's needs, regardless of their abilities and goals. Conant believed that this was particularly important in a time when attempts were being made to eliminate educational inequities, especially in segregated school districts. *Photo reproduced by permission of Archive Photos, Inc.*

Erik Erikson (1902–1994) Erik Erikson is best-known for investigating the manner in which psychology influences the learning process. He charted the development of the individual from infancy and early childhood on, pointing out that each stage of a young person's life is associated with specific psychological struggles that affect the individual's personality. During the 1960s, Erikson conducted behavioral research and published such influential texts as *Insight and Responsibility* (1964) and *Identity: Youth and Crisis* (1968). Educational theory was significantly influenced by his studies of children and adolescents, his conviction that human potential was boundless, and his belief that adults could overcome their childhood hardships.

Arthur Jensen (1923–) Arthur Jensen, a professor at the University of California, Berkeley, caused a firestorm in 1969 when he published a 123-page article in the *Harvard Educational Review*. Jensen alleged that genetics, rather than environment, was the key factor in determining an individual's IQ. Jensen offered a detailed study of how he came to this conclusion. Nonetheless, the popular press reduced his research to a flat statement: According to IQ test results, blacks were genetically inferior to whites. While education theorists appreciated the scholarly effort Jensen put into his study, almost everyone disagreed with his conclusion. *Photo reproduced by permission of AP/Wide World Photos.*

Francis Keppel (1916–1990) Francis Keppel established Harvard University's Graduate School of Education as a leader in innovative teacher training. He revised the Master of Arts in Teaching (MAT) degree, and originated the School and University Program for Research and Development (SUPRAD), which conducted experimental projects involving team teaching and other groundbreaking methods. In 1962, Keppel became the U.S. Commissioner of Education, and he labored to expand federal support of education. One of his most significant accomplishments involved the establishment of the National Assessment of Educational Progress (NAEP), a program that measures educational advances on a national level.

B. F. Skinner (1904–1990) B. F. Skinner devised new ways to teach everything from introductory psychology in college to introductory algebra in junior high schools based on his studies of how and why individuals act as they do, and his observation of the role of trial and error in education. Skinner was best known for his philosophy of human nature and learning. He believed learning consists of behavioral changes that occur as a result of a person's interaction with the properties and conditions of the physical and social environment. This contact shapes who we are and how we respond to the world. *Photo courtesy of the Archives of the History of American Psychology.*

◆ *Topics in the News* . . . .

❖ BILINGUAL EDUCATION

In previous eras, those who emigrated to the United States had readily learned to speak English. Whether their native languages were Yiddish, Polish, or Italian, they yearned to fit into American society. One way to accomplish this was by speaking English.

Beginning in the 1960s, this view radically changed among the new waves of immigrants. Many believed that abandoning their native languages would lead to severing connections with their native cultures. In 1967, an amendment was introduced to the Elementary and Secondary Education Act of 1965 providing for the establishment and promotion of bilingual education programs. The goals of the legislation included the cultivation of ancestral pride among youngsters and the reinforcement of their native languages.

Bilingual education was a sheer necessity in such locales as Miami, Florida, where waves of Cuban refugees were arriving and entering the school system. Non-Spanish-speaking teachers in Dade County struggled to communicate with their students. Many educators began attending night classes to learn to speak Spanish, while the school system hired former Cuban teachers as classroom assistants and translators.

In the face of this increased emphasis on bilingual education, critics complained that such programs do little more than ghettoize immigrants and prevent them from entering the American mainstream.

❖ THE CHANGING CURRICULUM

During the 1960s, students at all education levels studied newly offered subjects. The National Defense Education Act, whose content had been expanded from its original 1958 version, resulted in an increase in foreign-language classes. By 1966, more than three thousand college undergraduates were enrolled in courses offering intensive instruction in thirty-six languages. Many of those who successfully completed them went on to teach foreign languages in secondary schools.

The emerging civil rights movement and growing conflict over Vietnam led to changes in the study and teaching of American history. Previously, the American past had been portrayed as being completely glorious. Pioneers who "settled" the American West were presented as courageous, forward-thinking individuals who helped build a great nation by stretching their country's borders from the Atlantic to the Pacific. The fact that

The Degeneration of the English Language

In a 1964 article published in *Newsweek* magazine, writers and educators lamented the demise of standard English. Humorist-cartoonist James Thurber (1894–1961) was quoted on the subject. Before he died, Thurber bemoaned the "spreading malaise of 'you know' as well as do wop choruses, bop talk, slang, intellectualese, government jargon, and sloppy grammar." All, according to Thurber, were "continually eroding the king's English." Added Northwestern University professor Dwight Macdonald, (1906–1982), "When the typical student commits his thoughts to writing, he defiles his own language."

Attendees at the annual conference of the National Council of Teachers that year suggested all current English teachers be retrained. The College Board Commission on English proposed a different solution: more classroom writing assignments and an increase in classic literature on student booklists.

Native American tribes were displaced and often unfairly treated by the U.S. government was ignored. At a 1969 conference sponsored by the American Historical Association, Yale University historian C. Vann Woodward (1908–1999) observed, "Was the U.S. record all that righteous, unique, and pure, or is this a national illusion?"

In 1955, Woodward had authored *The Strange Career of Jim Crow,* in which he charted the history of segregation. Martin Luther King Jr. (1929–1968), the era's preeminent civil rights leader, called Woodward's book "the historical bible of the Civil Rights movement." At the same time, historian, social critic, and future Librarian of Congress Daniel Boorstin (1914–) emphasized that students needed to be exposed to history as experienced by all segments of society. He noted that students should "frankly face the role of violence and oppression in our history." Such sentiments in the late 1950s influenced the development in the 1960s of new fields of historical study such as black history, urban history, and, as the feminist movement grew during the 1970s, women's studies.

Social science and sociology, the study of the interaction that occurs and problems that arise when people live together as social groups, was another new and popular scholastic discipline. Between 1963 and 1965, student enrollment in graduate programs in sociology at the University of

Southern California (USC) doubled. "Young people today are very concerned with catastrophic changes that are leaving people bruised and broken," noted the dean of the School of Social Welfare at the University of California at Los Angeles (UCLA).

Theater arts was another emerging field of study. Before the 1960s, aspiring performers had to go to New York to attend acting school, where they would hope to break into the profession. However, in 1959, UCLA brought a professional acting troupe to its campus to establish a theater. During the 1960s, dozens of universities established drama programs for the purpose of training actors for Broadway and regional theaters. Eventually, universities constructed dazzling new state-of-the-art theaters. The $20 million Krannert Center for Performing Arts, at the University of Illinois, was completed in 1966. Because they were supported by the universities and not dependent for their survival on ticket sales, they did not have to show mainstream productions. Instead, they were able to encourage experimentation and creativity.

Innovations in teaching at the primary and secondary school level were not limited to new subject matter; familiar areas of study were taught in new ways. Linguists, theorists, and scholars developed new methods for teaching English, math, and science. Subjects were taught by engaging the student's imagination and intellectual curiosity, rather than by rote. Teacher-led discussions encouraged students to develop their minds, ask questions about the subject matter, and arrive at their own conclusions. Students were encouraged to explore ideas rather than memorize facts.

Such "learning by discovery" approaches, while heartily endorsed by many educators and students, also met with controversy. Some veteran teachers were displeased, because this new approach required additional preparation and effort; it veered from the traditional manner of teaching, which had as its focus a specific set of facts and ideas that students were expected to memorize and prove mastery of through tests and other objective measures. Some parents, noting that their children were not committing facts to memory as they had done, complained the education system was failing.

❖ THE DRAFT AND VIETNAM

In 1965, as the war in Vietnam escalated, nineteen-year-olds were being conscripted into the military and draft deferments for married men were abolished. However, deferments remained in place for all matriculated university students. College became a haven for avoiding Vietnam, and a young male who dropped out of school or was asked to leave because of failing grades more than likely wound up in the military. At the time, an

Amherst College professor joked that the school's new grading system consisted of five classifications: A (excellent); B (good); C (fair); D (passing); and V (Vietnam). Explained a colleague at UCLA, "Fear is a driving force in academia these days. I am damned sure students are studying more."

During World War II, young Americans from all classes and educational backgrounds went into battle, side by side. Now, college-age men who otherwise might not continue their education beyond high school readily enrolled in college to avoid Vietnam. The result was that the war was being fought not by a cross-section of Americans, but by the working class and poor who could not afford to enter college. Those from the middle or upper classes had sufficient financial resources to pay tuition fees and buy their way out of (or at least postpone) serving in the military.

❖ EDUCATING THE MILITARY

In 1960, a military pilot incorrectly set his compass and flew over Canada, rather than California. A major's error in arithmetic resulted in a fuel miscalculation and the landing of a jet fleet at the wrong airfield. Such mistakes were disturbing to the military's top brass. If a lack of education could foul up a simple peacetime exercise, what might happen during wartime? Would battles and lives be lost because of mathematical error or failure to understand instructions?

To combat this problem, the U.S. military appropriated $63 million to tutor its officers. By 1964, an education program was in full force, with hundreds of thousands of GIs returning to classrooms to study everything from basic reading, writing, and arithmetic to subjects at the postgraduate level.

The military's effort to educate its soldiers was not restricted to the upper ranks. The increase in college enrollments outside the military, coupled with the need for more manpower, resulted in the lowering of draft standards for recruits. Now, those with as low as a sixth-grade education qualified for the draft. Nevertheless, each year, one in every three of the 1.5 million men who turned twenty-one failed to meet the military's aptitude requirements. In response, the army initiated Project 100,000 (indicating the number of student-soldiers it hoped to enroll by 1968), a program that offered basic remedial courses leading to high-school equivalency degrees.

❖ EDUCATION FAULTFINDING

During the 1960s, Paul Goodman (1911–1972) earned fame as an outspoken critic of the manner in which Americans were educated. He argued that schools harmed, rather than improved, young people.

Montessori Schools

In the 1890s, Maria Montessori (1870–1952) was a medical student serving an internship in a psychiatric clinic in Rome. She was horrified by the manner in which the children were treated and began a lifelong study of mentally deficient youngsters. Eventually, her work included investigating the education of all children. Mostly, she worked with the poor, in whom she saw a vast potential that remained mostly untapped. Montessori's research resulted in her pioneering theories involving children and education. "All children are endowed with (the) capacity to 'absorb culture'," she explained. As such, they are able to learn naturally, employing creativity and spontaneity. Her belief was that a teacher's purpose was not to "instruct," but to make available learning opportunities to which each child might instinctively relate. Upon graduating medical school in 1896, Montessori became the first female physician in Italy. Eventually, she abandoned her work in medicine to work full-time as a children's education advocate.

Montessori's methods were not new in the 1960s. However, they attracted renewed interest with the 1964 republication of her 1912 book, *The Montessori Method: Scientific Pedagogy as Applied to Child Education in 'the Children's Houses'*. This rediscovery of Montessori and her theories resulted in the implementation of her methods into early childhood education programs.

In *Compulsory MisEducation*, his 1964 critique of formal education in the United States, Goodman wrote that Americans "already have too much formal schooling, and the more we get, the less education we will get." He added that "schools play a noneducational role—in the tender grades the schools are a baby-sitting service.... In the junior and senior grades, they are an arm of the police, providing cops and concentration camps paid for in the budget under the heading 'Board of Education.'"

Goodman believed that the primary purpose of the education "establishment" was not to arouse intellectual curiosity and teach students how to be independent thinkers. Rather, it was to "provide apprentice training for corporations, government, and the teaching profession itself, and to train the young to adjust to authority." While attending school did teach children how to interact with others, Goodman believed that school systems did little more than temporarily control the behavior of young people through external pressure in a structured setting. In a debate with Harvard University president James B. Conant (1893–1978), Goodman declared that such "regimentation" has "saddled us with an inhumane and uncitizenly society…"

Goodman pioneered the concept of the "open university": an unstructured "free university" where do-it-yourself learning was the rule. Upon publication of his 1966 book, *The Open University,* over a dozen American campuses established such programs. Huts were built on the campus of San Francisco State University, where various courses were available. Often, they were initiated and taught by students. At Cornell University, for example, Muslim students offered courses on Islamic culture. A professor even enrolled in a course on jazz history taught by one of his students.

Paul Goodman and his theories and criticisms were controversial and not accepted by the education establishment as a whole. However, he was a catalyst to open debate about the function and purpose of structured education opportunities in American society.

❖ FEDERAL ROLE IN EDUCATION

The 1960s saw an increase in the federal government's involvement in, and support of, educational programs. In 1961, Congress renewed the National Defense Education Act of 1958. Upon entering office in 1961, President John F. Kennedy (1917–1963) pushed for more federal aid to education. Controversy arose when Kennedy chose to support federal funding only for public schools; many Catholic politicians believed government monies also should be committed to parochial schools. Other regional office-holders, mostly Republicans and Southern Democrats, were firmly against federal educational funding. The reason: federal bills often included clauses involving school desegregation.

In December 1963, less than one month after Kennedy's assassination, his successor, Lyndon B. Johnson (1908–1973), signed into law the Higher Education Facilities Act of 1963. Johnson, like Kennedy, was dedicated to improving American education and increasing federal participation in education. In 1965, Johnson announced that he foresaw the United States becoming a "Great Society," a nation of plenty. In this "Great Society," all American children would be the beneficiaries of top-flight schooling. That year, U.S. Commissioner of Education Francis Keppel (1916–1990) described the federal government's new role in education as that of "a junior partner in a firm in which the major stockholders are the state, and local and private education agencies."

Before Johnson left office in 1969, a number of ambitious federal programs were in place. The Teacher Corps brought young people to urban slums and poor rural areas, where they worked as educators. The Head Start program attacked poverty by establishing educational programs for four- and five-year-old preschoolers. Follow Through served as a supple-

ment to Head Start. College students were guaranteed student loans; they could borrow up to $1,000 per year, begin repayment nine months after graduation, and have up to a decade to pay off the loan at 3 percent interest. Scholarships were available for many who otherwise could not afford college tuition. Work-study programs allowed undergraduates to combine classes with full-time summer and part-time fall and spring jobs with nonprofit organizations. Host groups provided 10 percent of the funding; the federal government contributed the remaining 90 percent. Other projects included increased funds for public television and aid for school and library construction. During Johnson's time in office, annual federal aid to education increased from $1.8 billion to over $12 billion.

❖ INTEGRATION OF PUBLIC SCHOOLS

At the beginning of the decade, the landmark *Brown* v. *Board of Education of Topeka, Kansas* Supreme Court decision was six years old. *Brown* v. *Board of Education* overruled the "separate but equal" doctrine with regard to schools; segregated public schools were judged to be unconstitutional. Nonetheless, particularly in the American South, many schools remained segregated. Often, local officials simply avoided the issue.

In 1964, the newly passed Civil Rights Act authorized the U.S. Office of Education to withhold federal funds from school systems that had failed to integrate. Plus, the U.S Attorney General was encouraged to legally enforce desegregation. At the beginning of the 1964 and 1965 school year, only 604 of 2,951 school districts in eleven Southern states had begun the desegregation process. One year later, 2,816 systems started the process. This change was a direct result of the threat of losing federal funding.

Still, a number of systems only made token efforts to integrate themselves. For example, some began a "freedom of choice" program, whereby students were allowed to select the schools they would attend. Occasionally, black students chose all-white ones, yet rarely if ever did a white child agree to switch to a predominantly black school. By the end of the decade, additional Supreme Court rulings had stripped Southern school districts of this kind of legal maneuvering. The court's position, once and for all, was that "the obligation of every school district is to terminate dual school systems at once and to operate now and hereafter only unitary systems."

Integration was not just a Southern issue. In states from New York to California, many schools were segregated simply because children from predominantly black or white neighborhoods attended schools in their communities. Busing students to different school districts seemed a logical solution. However, this approach proved controversial. In the New York

OPPOSITE PAGE
The March on Washington was a protest calling for the end of segregation in public schools, among other education and economic reforms. **Courtesy of the National Archives and Records Administration.**

The Morals Revolution

During the first half of the decade, college administrators were empowered to serve as the surrogate parents of undergraduates. In this regard, they had unquestioned authority over a student's personal life. For example, female students on many campuses had to adhere to nightly curfews, and sign in and out when leaving dormitories. Students were prohibited from visiting the dormitory rooms of members of the opposite sex.

These reins began to loosen during the late 1960s. Between 1955 and 1965, the number of college students nationwide increased from 2.5 million to 5.5 million. This rising population made it difficult for administrators to continue limiting student freedom. The sexual revolution also was changing on-campus attitudes. While chastity remained a virtue for many students, others were rethinking their positions on premarital sex.

Increasing pressure from students resulted in the termination of many dormitory regulations. However, not all administrators approved of these changes. Observed Theodore M. Hesburgh, president of the University of Notre Dame, "If anyone seriously believes he cannot become well-educated without girls in his room, he should get free of Notre Dame."

City borough of Manhattan, 2,700 Parent-Teacher Association (PTA) members vowed to contest school busing. One parent protested, "Why do our children have to be inconvenienced just to satisfy the Negroes' whims?"

❖ STUDENT UNREST

The tide of social unrest that swept across the United States during the 1960s had a direct bearing on university life. From mid-decade on, a revolution raged on campuses across America. College students were protesting everything from their nation's involvement in the war in Vietnam to what they believed was a lack of quality and relevance in the education they were receiving. Their activism produced changes in college curricula, student regulations, administrative policies, and the manner in which colleges related to their students.

In the early 1960s, college campuses were generally conservative in nature. The academic community had close links with government and defense contractors; many school administrators were federal bureaucrats and corporate executives rather than educators. At this time, school enrollments began to bulge as the baby boom generation reached college age. Many students and professional academics began to question the values their school's administrators appeared to represent.

The student protest movement rose from the Civil Rights movement. In the early 1960s, college students who were deeply committed to securing equality for black Americans traveled to the South and participated in voting rights drives. Back on their campuses throughout the country, they became more outspoken about other issues they perceived as unjust. The decade's first documented on-campus protest occurred in 1964 at the University of California, Berkeley, where a small dispute over school regulations exploded into a major confrontation. Berkeley was a major provider of military research. Not coincidentally, at the beginning of the 1964 and 1965 school year, students were informed they no longer could give political speeches or hand out literature involving social issues at the student union. While student civil rights activists viewed the edict as being aimed specifically at them, all student political organizations, whether liberal or conservative, stood to suffer from the ban.

Student protests, especially on college campuses, were common during the 1960s.
Reproduced by permission of the Corbis Corporation.

Mario Savio was a well-known student protestor at the University of California, Berkeley.
Reproduced by permission of Archive Photos, Inc.

On September 17, 1964, a coalition of campus groups calling itself the United Front petitioned the school administration to rescind the order. The Berkeley decision-makers refused to do so. One of the protest leaders was Mario Savio (1942–1996), a philosophy student who had spent the previous summer in Mississippi helping black sharecroppers to register to vote. Savio believed the edict restricted the constitutional right to free speech.

The policy served to unite students and make them active participants in what came to be known as the "free speech movement." In an address in which he attacked university president Clark Kerr (1911–), Savio noted, "An autocracy [dictatorship] runs this university…if President Kerr is the manager, then the faculty are a bunch of employees and we're the raw material. But we don't mean to be made into any product, don't mean to end up being bought by some clients of the university.… We're human beings." When a Berkeley official asserted that the ban would preserve political neutrality, Savio responded, "The University of California is directly involved in making new and better atom bombs. Whether this is good or bad, don't you think…in the spirit of political neutrality, either they should not be involved or there should be some democratic control over the way they're being involved?" In any case, for the protestors, the issue was about free speech, rather than political neutrality.

The dispute between the university and the demonstrators raged for several weeks. It culminated in December in a sit-in at Sproul Hall involving between eight hundred and one thousand students. (The "sit-in" was a tactic first employed in civil rights protests; it was a preplanned action in which a mass of individuals occupied seats in a segregated bus depot or restaurant, for the purpose of integrating it.) California governor Edmund G. "Pat" Brown (1905–1996) responded to the student protest by ordering six hundred police to clear the hall. In the end, 773 students were taken into custody, in what then was the largest mass-arrest in state history. In response, ten thousand students went on strike. They refused to attend classes and picketed the university's gates. Eventually, the school's faculty senate passed a resolution calling for the lifting of the ban. The Berkeley chancellor was relieved of his duties, and was replaced by an academic. The protesters' success at Berkeley encouraged similar demonstrations at other universities across the country. A year later, in 1965, movie actor-turned-politician Ronald Reagan (1911–), a conservative, was elected governor of California. He mustered enough votes to win by campaigning against the "sit-ins, teach-ins, and walk-outs" at Berkeley, and by promising to institute a "throw-out" within the university.

By 1965, when President Lyndon Johnson (1908–1973) began escalating the war in Vietnam, college students nationwide had a cause they could rally behind. As the years passed, increasing numbers of Americans of all ages and from all segments of society came to believe that military involvement in Vietnam was a mistake. However, at the outset, those who were vocally antiwar primarily were college students.

Throughout the rest of the 1960s and into the 1970s, the protest movement flourished on campuses. At Harvard in 1966, members of the

The Strawberry Statement

In 1968, nineteen-year-old Columbia University student protester James Simon Kunen (1948–) became a spokesperson for his generation when published *The Strawberry Statement: Notes of a College Revolutionary,* in which he offered his thoughts on the lifestyles and beliefs of contemporary youth.

"People want to know who we are," Kunen observed, "and some think they know who we are—a bunch of snot-nosed brats. It's difficult to say really who we are. We don't have snot on our noses. What we do have is hopes and fears."

Back in the late 1960s, long hair was not merely a hairstyle; it was often a symbol of one's political beliefs. Conservative Americans generally held a negative opinion of young men with long hair. In acknowledgment of that sentiment, Kunen noted, "as for bad vibrations emanating from my [hair] follicles, I say great. I want the cops to sneer and the old ladies swear and the businessmen worry. I want everyone to see me and say, 'There goes an enemy of the state,' because that's where I'm at, as we say in the Revolution biz."

Students for a Democratic Society (SDS), a radical group, scoffed at U.S. Defense Secretary Robert McNamara (1916–)and refused to allow his car to leave campus. Students at the University of Chicago staged a sit-in to protest on-campus examinations being conducted by the Selective Service System, the organization empowered to draft young men into the military. In 1967, students at the University of Wisconsin destroyed school property while protesting on-campus recruitment by Dow Chemical, a major defense contractor. The following year, students at Columbia University occupied several campus building for eight days. They were protesting Vietnam war-related research at the university, the school's ownership of slum buildings in the nearby Harlem community, and the school's attempt to construct a gymnasium on the site of a Harlem park.

On various occasions hundreds of thousands of students from across the nation came to Washington, D.C. to protest their country's Vietnam policies. Meanwhile, black students were demanding concessions from universities, including increases in black administrators and professors and black studies courses.

Clashes between students and authorities sometimes turned violent and deadly. In May 1970, months of antiwar protest on the campus of Kent State University in Ohio ended with the Ohio National Guard shooting into a crowd of demonstrators. Four students were killed, and nine others were wounded.

For More Information

BOOKS

Bode, Janet. *The Colors of Freedom: Immigrant Stories*. New York: Franklin Watts, 1999.

Haskins, James. *Separate, but Not Equal: The Dream and the Struggle*. New York: Scholastic, 1998.

Lusane, Clarence. *The Struggle for Equal Education*. New York: Franklin Watts, 1992.

Rasmussen, R. Kent. *Farewell Jim Crow: The Rise and Fall of Segregation in America*. New York: Facts on File, 1997.

Walter, Mildred Pitts. *Mississippi Challenge*. New York: Bradbury Press, 1992.

WEB SITES

Bilingual Education. http://ourworld.compuserve.com/homepages/ JWCRAWFORD/biling.htm (accessed on August 6, 2002).

Whatever Happened to Integration? www.theatlantic.com/issues/97feb/integ.htm (accessed on August 6, 2002).

chapter four # Government, Politics, and Law

1960: **May 5** A U-2 spy plane is shot down over Soviet territory, launching a crisis between the United States and Soviet Union, which results in the cancellation of a U.S.-Russian summit meeting.

1960: **May 6** The 1960 Civil Rights Act becomes law.

1960: **September 26** Presidential nominees Democrat John F. Kennedy and Republican Richard M. Nixon meet for the first-ever televised debate between presidential candidates.

1960: **November 8** John F. Kennedy is elected president.

1960: **December** Kennedy names his brother Robert as U.S. attorney general.

1961: **January 3** The United States breaks off diplomatic relations with Cuba.

1961: **March 13** President Kennedy proposes that the United States and Latin American countries form an "Alliance for Progress" to promote economic and social reform and prevent the spread of communism.

1961: **April 17** Cuban exiles invade Cuba at the Bay of Pigs. They are defeated by April 20.

1961: **May 4** The Freedom Riders begin traveling throughout the American South to counteract racism and segregation.

1961: **August 13** Communist East Germany closes its borders with West Berlin and begins building the Berlin Wall.

1962: **October 22** President Kennedy announces the presence of Soviet missiles in Cuba. The resulting crisis ends one week later.

1963: **July 25** The United States, Soviet Union, and Great Britain sign the Partial Nuclear Test Ban Treaty.

1963: **August 28** Martin Luther King Jr. gives his famous "I Have a Dream" speech in Washington, D.C.

1963: **September 15** Four little girls are killed when a black Birmingham, Alabama, church is bombed.

1963: **November 1** South Vietnamese President Ngo Dinh Diem and his family are murdered in a U.S.-backed coup.

1963: **November 22** President Kennedy is assassinated in Dallas. Vice President Lyndon Johnson becomes the new chief executive.

1964: **January 8** In his State of the Union message, President Johnson declares a "War on Poverty."

1964: **June 14** The United Steelworkers of America union and eleven major steel companies sign an agreement to end racial discrimination in the industry.

1964: **July 2** The Civil Rights Act of 1964 becomes law.

1964: **July 18** Riots break out in New York City's Harlem and Brownsville, and spread to other cities.

1964: **September 30** President Johnson signs the Equal Opportunity Act, providing funding for youth programs, antipoverty measures, and small business loans.

1965: **February 21** Black nationalist leader Malcolm X is assassinated.

1965: **March 7** Alabama state and local police attack civil rights marchers in Selma, Alabama.

1965: **June 8** President Johnson authorizes American troops to engage in direct combat operations in Vietnam.

1965: **August 6** The 1965 Voting Rights Act becomes law.

1965: **August 11** Large-scale riots break out in Watts, a black Los Angeles neighborhood.

1965: **October 15** Anti-Vietnam War demonstrations occur in forty U.S. cities.

1966: **January** Kentucky becomes the first southern state to pass a civil rights law.

1968: **January 30** North Vietnam launches a major attack known as the Tet Offensive.

1968: **March 10** U.S. soldiers kill hundreds of Vietnamese civilians in the My Lai Massacre.

1968: **April 4** Martin Luther King Jr. is assassinated in Memphis, Tennessee.

1968: **April 11** The Civil Rights Act of 1968 becomes law.

1968: **May 12** U.S.-North Vietnamese peace talks begin in Paris.

1968: **June 4** Robert Kennedy is assassinated.

1968: **August** Police battle protesters outside the Democratic National Convention in Chicago.

1968: **November 5** Richard M. Nixon is elected president.

1969: **April 3** American combat casualties in Vietnam since January 1, 1961, reach 33,641. This is 12 more than died in the Korean War.

1969: **July 8** The first U.S. troop reductions in Vietnam begin.

1969: **November 15** A quarter-of-a-million antiwar protesters march on Washington, D.C.

Overview

The decade of the 1960s has been called one of the most turbulent in all of American history. Several major events shaped the era: the assassination of U.S. President John F. Kennedy; the killings of other national leaders, including Martin Luther King Jr., Robert Kennedy, and Malcolm X, and controversies and crises surrounding the cold war with the Soviet Union, the surging Civil Rights movement, and the escalating war in Vietnam.

The decade began with much promise and hope on the national political scene, with the election of a young, vibrant new president. However, America faced both foreign and domestic challenges. The cold war carried over from the previous decade and the 1962 Cuban missile crisis almost resulted in a full-scale nuclear war between the United States and the Soviet Union. Black Americans pushed for equal rights and were met with violent resistance on the part of Southern segregationists (people who supported the separation of the races). Then in 1963, on a November day in Dallas, President Kennedy was murdered, sending the nation into mourning.

Vice President Lyndon Johnson followed Kennedy as chief executive. Johnson envisioned America as a "Great Society," one in which federal government-sponsored social programs would eradicate poverty. Johnson's "Great Society" and "War on Poverty," however well intentioned, were ill-fated. On one level, government funds used for antipoverty programs did little more than set up federal bureaucracies. Antipoverty programs were expensive to run and, in the end, did little to uplift the nation's poor, and funding for these programs had to be diverted to pay for the escalating war in Vietnam.

Furthermore, Johnson encountered trouble with his Vietnam policy. In an attempt to halt the spread of communism in Southeast Asia, the president began sending troops in increasing numbers to fight in the rice paddies of Vietnam. Almost immediately, Americans began protesting this action. Year by year, the numbers of protestors increased significantly.

By 1968, Americans were deeply concerned about the fate of their country. To many, it seemed that the great American experiment in democracy was coming apart and was doomed to failure. That year witnessed a seemingly unending string of crises both foreign and domestic. On the international front, North Korean communists seized the USS *Pueblo*, a U.S. Navy freighter sailing in international waters. The communist North Vietnamese launched the Tet Offensive, a military action that served notice that the war in Vietnam would not be easily won. American soldiers no longer were the good guys; in the small South Vietnamese village of My Lai, they massacred hundreds of civilians. On the domestic front, antiwar protests did not let up. The nation was split down the middle, between those who intoned such expressions as "America, love it or leave it" and "My country right or wrong," and those who responded by avowing "Hell, no, we won't go" to Vietnam. Two leading national figures, Martin Luther King Jr., and Robert Kennedy, were assassinated. President Johnson declared he would not seek his party's presidential nomination. Blood was spilled on the streets of Chicago during the Democratic National Convention, as police clubbed and tear-gassed antiwar protesters.

That year, Richard Nixon was the Republican presidential nominee. During the 1950s, Nixon was the two-term vice president under Dwight Eisenhower; in 1960, he lost the presidency to Kennedy. This time around, Nixon defeated his Democratic opponent, Hubert Humphrey. By the end of the decade, Nixon presided over a country in which antiwar protests grew larger and louder and more frequent. Yet despite troop withdrawals from Vietnam, the American presence in Southeast Asia continued into the 1970s and civil unrest continued.

Lyndon B. Johnson (1908–1973) Texan Lyndon B. Johnson, a former powerhouse in Congress, became the U.S. vice president in 1961, with the swearing-in of John F. Kennedy. Upon Kennedy's assassination in 1963, Johnson was elevated to chief executive. With the federal legislation that accompanied his vision of America as a "Great Society," Johnson ambitiously tried to erase poverty and other problems of society. However, over the course of time, most of his programs failed. His decreasing popularity, stemming from the growing protests over his escalation of the war in Vietnam, led to his decision not to seek his party's presidential nomination in 1968. *Photo reproduced by permission of AP/Wide World Photos.*

John F. Kennedy (1917–1963) John F. Kennedy was the youngest man, and the first Roman Catholic, elected to the U.S. presidency. The Massachusetts Democrat won a Senate seat in 1952. He almost won his party's vice-presidential nod in 1956, before being elected as president four years later. Kennedy was assassinated in November 1963, barely three years after becoming president. *Photo reproduced courtesy of the Library of Congress.*

Robert Kennedy (1925–1968) Robert Kennedy, the younger brother and close confidante of President John F. Kennedy, served as U.S. attorney general in the Kennedy administration. In 1964, after his brother's death, Kennedy won a New York senate seat. He quickly became one of the Democratic Party's leading liberal spokespeople, and in 1968 he mounted a campaign to win his party's presidential nomination. However, that June, after earning a victory in the California primary election, he, too, was felled by an assassin's bullet. *Photo reproduced courtesy of the National Archives and Records Administration.*

Martin Luther King Jr. (1929–1968) Martin Luther King Jr. became a symbol of the outcry for equal rights that echoed throughout America during the 1950s and 1960s. A Baptist preacher, King helped form the Southern Christian Leadership Conference (SCLC). His shining moment came during the 1963 March on Washington, when he gave his stirring "I Have a Dream" speech. A year later, he was awarded the Nobel Peace Prize. King emphasized nonviolent protest as a means of securing racial equality. However, in April 1968, he was assassinated in Memphis, Tennessee, where he had gone to support striking sanitation workers. *Photo reproduced by permission of Archive Photos, Inc.*

Eugene McCarthy (1916–) From the mid-1960s on, Democratic Senator Eugene McCarthy of Minnesota was a leading voice in the anti-Vietnam War movement. He came to view the war as "morally unjustified," and in 1968 became a presidential candidate. McCarthy believed he had no hope of winning the nomination, let alone the election. However, his strong showing in the New Hampshire primary reflected the growing discontent over the Vietnam polices of incumbent Lyndon Johnson. During the 1968 Democratic national convention, McCarthy's supporters staged an angry, and unsuccessful, floor fight for the addition of an antiwar policy item to the party's platform. *Photo reproduced courtesy of the Library of Congress.*

Richard M. Nixon (1913–1994) In the 1960s, Richard M. Nixon lost the presidency in a close election against John F. Kennedy. Then in 1962, Edmund G. "Pat" Brown (1905–1996) soundly defeated him in the California governor's race. In defeat, Nixon claimed that the press no longer would "have Nixon to kick around anymore," because "this is my last press conference." However, Nixon was destined to preside over many more press conferences. He campaigned for his party's 1968 presidential nomination and ended up winning the presidential election. Nixon eventually resigned from office in the aftermath of the Watergate scandal in 1974. *Photo reproduced by permission of the Corbis Corporation.*

George C. Wallace (1919–1998) Of all the Southern politicians who garnered national attention for their fervent opposition to integration, Alabama governor George C. Wallace was the most high-profile. It was Wallace's vow to uphold "segregation now—segregation tomorrow—and segregation forever" that earned him national headlines. After running in Democratic Party primaries during the 1964 presidential campaign, Wallace emerged as a full-fledged candidate four years later. He was a third-party candidate, and he won 13.5 percent of the vote. In May 1972, Wallace was shot and partially paralyzed by a gunman who allegedly shot him in order to become famous. *Photo reproduced by permission of the Corbis Corporation.*

❖❖ **Topics in the News** . . . .

❖ CIVIL RIGHTS

The civil rights protests and boycotts of the 1950s exploded in number during the 1960s as more and more people joined efforts to end racial discrimination. Such well-established organizations as the National Association for the Advancement of Colored People (NAACP), and newly established ones such as the Southern Christian Leadership Conference (SCLC), worked to tear down racism. These groups employed legal means and nonviolent resistance. Efforts to integrate public schools flooded school districts with lawsuits. African Americans seated themselves at "whites-only" lunch counters and refused to leave until served. By the end of 1960, some 70,000 had participated in such demonstrations in 150 cities and towns. Over 3,600 had been arrested. Joining them were the Freedom Riders: groups of black and white Americans who traveled by bus across the South and tested Supreme Court desegregation rulings and similar federal legislation.

Democrat John F. Kennedy (1917–1963), who was elected president in 1960, campaigned on a promise to push through additional civil rights initiatives. While the Democrats controlled Congress, those in power were conservative Southerners who wanted no part of such legislation. However, the mounting, often violent resistance to civil rights laws spurred Kennedy into action. In February 1963, he sent a message to Congress asking for more legislation.

Martin Luther King Jr. (1929–1968), became the era's high-profile civil rights leader. In 1963, he led a protest in Birmingham, Alabama, one of the most segregated cities in America. From 1957 through 1963, Birmingham was the site of eighteen racially motivated bombing incidents and fifty cross burnings; the city's police force had a reputation for harassment of the black community. During the protest, King was arrested and jailed and police dogs were unleashed on demonstrators. In the following weeks, hundreds of civil rights demonstrations were mounted across the South. All culminated in August with a massive national "March on Washington," the purpose of which was to lobby Congress to support President Kennedy's civil rights initiatives.

Five days after the Kennedy assassination, his successor, Lyndon Johnson (1908–1973), asked Congress for the earliest possible passage of the slain president's civil rights package. The Civil Rights Act of 1964 passed the House and was sent on to the Senate, where conservative Southerners conducted a forty-seven-day-long filibuster (delaying of leg-

"I Have a Dream"

During the August 1963 "March on Washington," Martin Luther King Jr. gave his celebrated "I Have a Dream" speech. In it, he proclaimed his vision of equality, a time when his four children would "not be judged by the color of their skin but by the content of their character." He yearned for a world in which "all of God's children, black men and white men, Jews and Gentiles, Protestants and Catholics, will be able to join hands and sing in the words of the old Negro spiritual, 'Free at last! Free at last! Thank God Almighty, we are free at last!'"

islative action by means of excessively long speechmaking), the longest in Senate history. In June, the Senate voted to cut off debate. The bill passed, and was signed into law. Among its provisions, it outlawed racial discrimination in public accommodations and gave the U.S. Justice Department increased powers to push for school desegregation.

Voting rights was another key issue. Throughout the South, many blacks had never registered to vote because they were intimidated by literacy tests or fearful of job loss and threats of violence. In 1961, civil rights organizations initiated voting rights campaigns. Volunteers poured into Southern communities to conduct adult-literacy classes and walk blacks through the voter registration process.

Lyndon Johnson's landslide victory in the 1964 presidential race carried enough liberal Democrats into Congress to break the conservative stranglehold over civil rights legislation. The result was passage of the Voting Rights Act of 1965, which outlawed literacy requirements for voters and empowered federal authorities to take control of the voter-registration process where discrimination existed.

❖ THE COLD WAR AND THE SOVIETS

The cold war was an ideological conflict pitting the United States and its Western allies against the Soviet Union and other communist-governed nations. During the previous decade, both sides increased production of nuclear bombs and the hardware necessary to launch them. Continuing into the 1960s, each side kept developing and building these instruments of war. Although the cold war continued with the same high intensity and antagonism that existed in the 1950s, a number of meetings between the two superpowers did occur throughout the 1960s. Among the major subjects under discussion were banning nuclear testing and controlling the race to build new weapons, also called the "arms race."

The decade's first cold war-related crisis came in May 1960, when an American U-2 spy plane was shot down in Soviet airspace. President Dwight Eisenhower (1890–1969) initially denied that the United States conducted aerial spying missions over the Soviet Union. However, he had to admit the truth when the Russians put on display the captured pilot, Francis Gary Powers (1929–1977). Nevertheless, Eisenhower refused to apologize to the Soviets and defended the missions. A planned summit meeting between the two nations was canceled.

❖ THE COLD WAR: THE BAY OF PIGS AND THE CUBAN MISSILE CRISIS

As relations between the United States and the Soviet Union remained tense, an additional threat to U.S. security emerged. This peril appeared just ninety miles from the southern tip of the state of Florida.

In January 1959, a revolutionary group led by Fidel Castro (1926–) overthrew the corrupt dictatorship of Fulgencio Batista (1901–1973) in Cuba. Castro proved to be no U.S. ally. In February 1960, he signed diplomatic and trade agreements with the Soviet Union. Then in June, he seized American-operated oil refineries in Cuba. Three months later, Castro attended a United Nations session in New York, at which time he publicly embraced Nikita Khrushchev (1894–1971), the Soviet premier. Eventually, Castro dictated that the Cuban Communist Party was the island's lone legitimate political party.

In 1960, the Central Intelligence Agency (CIA) began secretly training a force of Cuban exiles. The agency also concocted a plan to have them invade Cuba, at the Bay of Pigs. After becoming president the following year, John F. Kennedy ordered the invasion to proceed. The action was a major catastrophe. CIA intelligence reports were in error, and after three days all the invaders were killed or captured.

Then in August 1962, intelligence reports confirmed that Russian ships were transporting military personnel and weapons to Cuba. At the beginning of September, the Soviets declared that they planned to supply more military resources in order to counteract an alleged American threat to Cuba. U.S. spy planes observed antiaircraft missile sites under construction on the island. From these sites, a nuclear attack could have been launched against Washington, D.C. It was determined that the sites would be operational by the end of October.

Kennedy and his advisors considered several strategies, including secret talks and public negotiations with the Soviets, private talks with Fidel Castro, and an air strike, invasion, or naval blockade (preventing passage in and out) of Cuba. After speaking to congressional leaders on October 22, Kennedy informed the nation of the situation in a dramatic televised speech. He warned that a missile attack would be met with an appropriate military response. He demanded that the Soviets remove the missiles, and then imposed a blockade of Cuba. The Soviets first responded by condemning Kennedy's action and accusing him of pushing civilization to the brink of nuclear war. Then they agreed to remove the missiles under United Nations supervision. Yet just as quickly, they amended this promise, claiming they only would do so if the United States removed its nuclear missiles from Turkey. U.S. intelligence also reported that Soviet embassy officials in New York had begun destroying sensitive documents, a step usually undertaken at the start of a war.

At the suggestion of Attorney General Robert Kennedy (1925–1968), the United States ignored the last message, and responded in a positive manner only to the one before it. The strategy worked. President Kennedy announced that the blockade would end only when the missile removal and launch site dismantling could be verified. Subsequent photo reconnaissance revealed that the Soviets acted as they had promised. On November 21, the blockade was lifted.

The realization of the events that had transpired had a sobering effect on the leaders of both nations, and a positive impact on how they interacted in the future. During the spring of 1963, the United States, Soviet Union, and Great Britain resumed talks about banning above-ground nuclear tests, negotiations that previously had been abandoned. In August, the three countries signed a treaty outlawing testing in the atmosphere, in outer space, and underwater. Another factor adding to a decrease in U.S.-Soviet Union tensions was the heightened hostility between the Soviets and communist China.

❖ ESCALATING INVOLVEMENT IN VIETNAM

In the early 1960s, increased communist rebellions in Southeast Asia were a source of concern for the United States. Since 1954, Vietnam—a narrow, S-shaped, 1,000-mile-long country—had been divided into communist North Vietnam and noncommunist South Vietnam. American foreign policy with relation to Vietnam may be explained by the "domino theory," which argued that if South Vietnam were to fall to the communists, then all of Southeast Asia would follow, just like a row of dominoes.

In the 1950s, American military advisors traveled to South Vietnam to train its military. At the time of President John F. Kennedy's assassination, 12,000 advisors were deployed in Vietnam; this number increased to 23,000 by the end of the year. The U.S. effort was costing $400 million per year, and by the end of 1963, seventy Americans had lost their lives in Vietnam.

However, the South Vietnamese government was becoming increasingly unstable. Three weeks before Kennedy's death, the South Vietnamese military overthrew and murdered the country's president, Ngo Dinh Diem (1901–1963). In the wake of attacks by North Vietnamese torpedo boats on U.S. destroyers in the Gulf of Tonkin in August 1964, Lyndon Johnson, Kennedy's successor, put before the U.S. Congress the Gulf of Tonkin Resolution. The resolution gave Johnson the power to take measures to repel further aggression without congressional approval. History has cited the resolution's passage as the beginning of full-scale U.S. military involvement in Vietnam.

The U.S. role in Vietnam soon shifted from providing assistance and military advisers to active combat. With this policy change came massive increases in troops. In July 1965, President Johnson announced that American troop levels were to be increased from 75,000 to 125,000. Almost two years later to the day, the military announced that, by the end of 1968, the American troop numbers were to climb to 525,000. By the end of 1967, approximately 15,000 GIs had been killed in Vietnam. One month into 1968, North Vietnam launched a surprise attack on the South, which came to be known as the Tet Offensive because it was launched during Tet, the Vietnamese holiday celebrating the lunar new year. The fighting that took place during the Tet Offensive was a signal that the war would not be won as easily as U.S. officials had led the public to believe.

As the number of American soldiers sent to Vietnam increased, so did concern by many American citizens about the American presence in Vietnam. The United States became a nation emotionally and politically divided. On one side were those who believed that the United States should not be engaged in Vietnam's internal conflict. On the other were those who firmly defended Johnson's policy, believing that the United States had an obligation to prevent the spread of communism in Southeast Asia. Antiwar activists were not content to quietly voice their protests. On April 17, 1965, between 15,000 and 25,000 demonstrated in Washington against the U.S. bombing of North Vietnam. Two years later, a crowd estimated to be between 100,000 and 400,000 heard Martin Luther King Jr. denounce

My Lai Massacre

In March 1968, three platoons—Company C, First Battalion, and 11th Brigade, American Division—entered the South Vietnamese village of My Lai (pronounced mee-LIE). They were on a search-and-destroy mission, in which they were to seek out and kill the enemy: the Viet Cong, communist guerilla fighters for North Vietnam. (Viet Cong, sometimes spelled Viet-cong, was shortened from *Viet Nam Cong San,* which meant People's Liberation Armed Forces in South Vietnam.)

The American soldiers found no Viet Cong in My Lai. However, before they left, hundreds of unarmed civilians, including women, children, and elderly men, were murdered. There was one U.S. casualty: a GI who had shot himself in the foot to avoid partaking in the slaughter.

Eventually, the U.S. Army launched an inquiry into what had happened at My Lai. Lieutenant William L. Calley Jr. (1943–), an inexperienced young officer, was charged with 102 counts of murder. He was court-martialed and convicted; his sentence of life in prison was eventually reduced to ten years, and he was paroled in 1974.

the war at a New York rally. On October 21, 1967, 100,000 anti-Vietnam demonstrators marched on Washington, D.C. Other large-scale protests followed. As time passed, increasing numbers of Americans came to view the war as a folly.

In 1968, America's Vietnam strategy changed from the pursuit of total military victory to an attempt to fashion a diplomatic solution that would allow the United States to remove itself from the war. Preliminary peace talks between the United States and North Vietnamese began in Paris. Antiwar protests continued at home.

In 1969, Republican Richard M. Nixon, the newly elected president, began limited troop withdrawals. By then, U.S. casualties had topped 33,000. At the same time, Nixon began escalating the war by ordering a secret bombing campaign in neighboring Cambodia, which the North Vietnamese had been using as a sanctuary. The war in Vietnam continued into the 1970s. Eventually, more than 55,000 Americans lost their lives in combat.

New Journalism

The 1960s saw the rise in what came to be known as New Journalism, which blended true-life stories and events with more subjective writing techniques. Novels such as *In Cold Blood* (1966), by Truman Capote (1924–1984), which combined real events—in this case, grisly murders and a subsequent trial—were marketed as nonfiction. On newspaper and magazine pages, writers such as Tom Wolfe, Hunter S. Thompson, Gay Talese, and Jimmy Breslin abandoned objective, just-the-facts journalism. They wedded fictional writing styles with reporting and often included themselves in their pieces.

❖ CRIME AND PUNISHMENT

A range of crime stories grabbed the headlines during the 1960s. In 1959, two petty criminals, Richard Hickock (1931–1965) and Perry Smith (1928–1965), murdered four members of the Clutter family in their home outside Holcomb, Kansas. The killers were apprehended, tried and found guilty, and executed. What earned the crime and its aftermath lasting notoriety was a celebrated, best-selling book: *In Cold Blood* (1965), a nonfiction account written in crime novel-style by Truman Capote (1924–1984).

In 1966, Charles Whitman (1941–1966), an architectural engineering student at the University of Texas at Austin, climbed to the top of a tower that soared 307 feet above the campus. Then he used an array of firearms to shoot at pedestrians and police. Before he was himself killed, fifteen people lay dead and thirty-one were injured.

Between 1962 and 1964, thirteen women were murdered in Boston. The manner in which they died resulted in their killer being nicknamed "The Boston Strangler." Albert DeSalvo (1931–1973) eventually was arrested and incarcerated; he admitted his guilt to a fellow prisoner. DeSalvo was sentenced to life in prison. In 1973, he was murdered in his cell, and his killer never was identified. However, in 2001, newly discovered DNA evidence indicated that DeSalvo may not have been the Strangler!

Perhaps the most shocking of the decade's crime stories involved the gruesome 1969 mass murders of several people in Los Angeles, among them Sharon Tate (1943–1969), the actress wife of film director Roman Polanski (1933–). The perpetrators were a band of young followers of

Charles Manson (1934–), a small-time criminal. The grisly crimes were replayed in the next decade in *Helter Skelter,* a crime novel-like account written by Vincent Bugliosi, who prosecuted the case against Manson, as well as a television movie by the same name.

The 1960s saw the rise of a new type of criminal: the skyjacker. Skyjackers are individuals who commandeer an airliner and demand to be flown to a specific destination. During the 1960s, that location was often Cuba. The first skyjacking to Cuba took place in May 1961. Almost fifty others were successfully completed throughout the decade.

Also during the 1960s, several U.S. Supreme Court decisions altered the manner in which police and the courts dealt with criminal defendants. In the 1961 case of *Mapp* v. *Ohio,* the Court ruled that the states could not consider trial evidence that had been seized without a search warrant and in violation of the Constitution. Subsequent decisions further defined what constituted an illegal search. In 1963's *Gideon* v. *Wainright,* the Court determined that states must appoint legal counsel, or public defense attorneys, for all defendants who could not afford to hire their own, not just those facing the death penalty. The following year, in *Escobedo* v. *Illinois,* the Court ruled that persons who become prime suspects during criminal investigations have the right to an attorney; if they are denied this right, any confession subsequently obtained is inadmissible in court. Also in 1964, in *New York Times* v. *Sullivan,* the Court placed heavy burdens-of-proof on public official who instigated libel (defamation of character) lawsuits. In 1966's *Miranda* v. *Arizona,* the Court ruled that a crime suspect must be informed of his rights, including the "right to remain silent," before any police interrogation can take place.

❖ LYNDON JOHNSON'S "GREAT SOCIETY" AND "WAR ON POVERTY"

On May 22, 1964, President Lyndon Johnson (1908–1973) gave a commencement speech at the University of Michigan. At the time, the nation was enjoying economic prosperity. Yet in the speech, the president told the graduates, "For in your time we have the opportunity to move not only toward the rich society and the powerful society, but upward to the 'Great Society.' The 'Great Society' rests on abundance and liberty for all. It demands an end to poverty and racial injustice, to which we are totally committed in our time."

The president concluded,

> So, will you join in the battle to give every citizen the full equality which God enjoins and the law requires, whatever his belief, or race, or the color of his skin? Will you join in the battle to give every citizen an escape from the crushing weight of poverty? Will you join in the battle to

make it possible for all nations to live in enduring peace—as neighbors and not as mortal enemies? Will you join in the battle to build the 'Great Society,' to prove that our material progress is only the foundation on which we will build a richer life of mind and spirit?

Following the speech, Johnson began what became popularly known as the "War on Poverty." Under his predecessor, a range of antipoverty measures had already become law. Economic development grants were available to communities in depressed regions. Low-cost loans benefited businesses that agreed to relocate to these communities. Federal funds had been set aside for home building and slum clearance. Workers whose jobs had become obsolete were to be provided with retraining. Johnson's domestic agenda included Medicare and Medicaid, which established a compulsory hospital-care program for the elderly. It increased federal aid to elementary and secondary schools, and provided scholarships and low-interest loans to college students. It funded rent supplements and construction costs for low-income housing. It protected consumer interest by mandating "truth-in-labeling" for consumer products and safety standards for automobiles, toys, and household items.

By the end of 1966, Johnson was forced to cut back on his "Great Society" and "War on Poverty" programs, because additional funding was needed to fight an altogether different war: the then-escalating one in Vietnam. Furthermore, critics of Kennedy's and Johnson's programs maintained that many of them created additional federal bureaucracies while doing little to improve the quality of life of their intended beneficiaries.

❖ NATIONAL POLITICS: ELECTION 1960

As the 1960 presidential campaign neared, one thing was certain: Republican President Dwight Eisenhower (1890–1969), a two-term incumbent, would not be running for reelection. Richard M. Nixon (1913–1994), Eisenhower's vice president, became the party's nominee. His opponent was Senator John F. Kennedy (1917–1963) of Massachusetts.

While Republican Party regulars and high-powered campaign funders favored Nixon, he faced a preprimary challenge from New York's Governor Nelson Rockefeller (1908–1979). Rockefeller eventually withdrew from the race, which then appeared to be an easy win for the vice president. Despite a "Draft Rockefeller" campaign that emerged after the U-2 spy plane incident, Nixon won the nomination after he and Rockefeller reached a compromise over the Republican Party platform.

In addition to Kennedy, three other major presidential hopefuls had emerged in the Democratic Party: Missouri Senator Stuart Symington (1901–1988), Texas Senator Lyndon Johnson (1908–1973), and Minnesota

Senator Hubert Humphrey (1911–1978). There even was a "Draft Stevenson" movement, with supporters urging that the nomination be handed to Adlai Stevenson (1900–1965). Though he was highly respected, Stevenson had lost the presidential election to Eisenhower in 1952 and 1956. Kennedy won the Democratic nomination, and chose Johnson as his running mate. In his acceptance speech, he declared that "the world is changing. The old era is ending.… (Americans are) standing on the edge of a New Frontier."

Key campaign issues included a strong defense against communism, which both candidates favored, as well as the economy and civil rights. Kennedy stressed the importance of public service and individual sacrifice, which he believed would lead the United States to new heights of domestic prosperity and international prestige.

One of the biggest hurdles blocking Kennedy's election was his religion. He was the second Roman Catholic ever to run for president. The first, New York Democratic Governor Alfred E. Smith (1873–1944), had been trounced by Herbert Hoover (1874–1964) in 1928. Helping Kennedy were his youth, his looks, and his vitality. A majority of those who saw his first televised debate with Nixon felt that Kennedy had won the debate;

Richard M. Nixon (left) and John F. Kennedy in the first nationally televised presidential debate. **Reproduced by permission of the Corbis Corporation.**

Eisenhower's Farewell

In January 1961, just before leaving office, President Eisenhower issued a warning that echoed through the decade and beyond. Cold war tensions were high, and the nation was clamoring for increased defense spending. Yet Eisenhower warned of the dangers posed by what he termed the growing "Military-Industrial Complex."

He explained that America had established "an immense military establishment and a large arms industry" that was "new to the American experience." This union, the outgoing president noted, could be catastrophic. Its

> "total influence—economic, political, even spiritual—is felt in every city, every statehouse, every office of the federal government.... In the councils of government we must guard against the acquisition of unwarranted influence, whether sought or unsought, by the Military-Industrial Complex. The potential for the disastrous rise exists and will persist."

Throughout the 1960s, these words were quoted more often than any others uttered by Eisenhower during his eight years in office. Anti-Vietnam War activists cited them when charging that the "Military-Industrial Complex" was running the country, as more of the nation's human and material resources were being employed to wage the war in Southeast Asia.

those who only heard the debate on radio judged Nixon the winner or thought the candidates had performed evenly. In November, the forty-one-year-old Kennedy won the general election. The results were extremely close, with 49.7 percent of the popular vote favoring Kennedy and 49.5 percent going to Nixon. Several days after being elected, Kennedy noted, "It was TV more than anything else that turned the tide."

In his now-legendary inauguration speech, Kennedy challenged Americans by declaring, "Ask not what your country can do for you. Ask what you can do for your country."

❖ PRESIDENTIAL POLITICS

During off-year elections, the party of the incumbent president usually loses seats in Congress. In 1962, the Republicans attacked Democratic President Kennedy's record on foreign policy. As the campaigning developed, one of the major issues was the escalating Cuban missile crisis. The Republicans charged that Kennedy had insufficiently responded to the increasing Soviet presence in Cuba. Republican politicians demanded that the president order an invasion of Cuba, or at least a naval blockade of the island, and they hoped to use the issue to support the election of more Republican senators and representatives.

However, Kennedy's successful handling of the crisis resulted in a Democratic gain in the Senate and a minimal loss in the House of Representatives. It was a far better outcome than the Democrats had expected.

November 22, 1963, became one of the darkest days in twentieth-century American history when President Kennedy was assassinated in Dallas. The nation was plunged into shock and mourning. Lyndon Johnson was sworn in as the new chief executive for the remainder of Kennedy's term of office. He then became the logical choice to represent his party in the 1964 presidential election. He did precisely that, despite a brief challenge from Alabama governor George Wallace (1919–1998), an outspoken and powerful opponent of racial integration, which Johnson's administration supported.

On the Republican side, Nelson Rockefeller again sought his party's nomination. He was the early frontrunner, but lost his bid to Arizona Senator Barry Goldwater (1909–1998), an archconservative. Rockefeller was a divorceé; his political undoing came in May 1963, when he married a divorced woman who had relinquished custody of her four children to her first husband. At the time, divorce in general was frowned upon in American society. For a politician seeking high office, it was disastrous.

The 1964 election was significant in Republican Party history. The party's conservative wing gained power over its more moderate Eastern establishment. During the campaign, the ultraconservative Goldwater was hurt by a number of off-the-cuff remarks he made, beginning with his declarations that Social Security payments should become voluntary and the United States should have dropped an atom bomb on North Vietnam a decade earlier. The Democrats portrayed him as a trigger-happy cowboy. They altered Goldwater's slogan, "In your heart you know he's right," to "In your heart you know he might," to suggest that his policies would be disastrous for the nation. Johnson, meanwhile, vowed to continue the political initiatives of his deceased predecessor, and attempted to place his own stamp on domestic policy with his battle cry for a "War on Poverty."

On Election Day, Johnson trounced Goldwater, winning 61.2 percent of the popular vote. The Democrats also made substantial gains in both houses of Congress. Presidential candidate Goldwater won only in Arizona and five southern states: Mississippi, Alabama, Louisiana, South Carolina, and Georgia.

After suffering national defeat in 1964, the Republicans came back strong two years later. While the Democrats maintained their House and Senate majorities, President Johnson lost the liberal mandate that supported and voted for his "Great Society" legislation. Much of the Republican's success in the midterm election of 1966 was due to Richard Nixon. The ex-vice president and failed presidential nominee actively campaigned cross-country for Republican candidates, and emerged as his party's leading spokesperson.

By 1968, much change had taken place in the United States. For one thing, the Vietnam War had escalated. Increasingly, Americans questioned both the American presence in Southeast Asia and the leadership of President Lyndon Johnson. Meanwhile, a revolt within the Democratic Party was brewing. By winning 42 percent of the vote in the New Hampshire presidential primary, Senator Eugene McCarthy (1916–) of Minnesota, who was staunchly against the war, was able to claim a moral victory. New York's Senator Robert Kennedy, certainly a familiar name in national politics, was also attracting Democratic voters.

On the last day of March 1968, Johnson delivered a televised address to the nation announcing that he had ordered a partial halt to the bombing of North Vietnam. He invited the North Vietnamese government in Hanoi to begin negotiating to end the war. Then, he dropped a bombshell. "I have concluded," he stated, "that I should not permit the Presidency to become involved in the partisan divisions that are developing in this political year.... Accordingly, I shall not seek and I will not accept the nomination of my party for another term as your President."

Public attention then focused on McCarthy and Kennedy, with the latter winning the all-important California primary in early June. Just moments after delivering his victory speech, however, he became the second Kennedy brother to be murdered by an assassin's bullet. In the aftermath, Hubert Humphrey, Johnson's vice president and the choice of party regulars, won the Democratic nomination. In order not to anger Johnson, Humphrey supported his Vietnam policies.

*OPPOSITE PAGE
Lyndon B. Johnson was
sworn in as the president
of the United States only
a short time after John F.
Kennedy's assassination.
Photo reproduced by
permission of AP/Wide
World Photos.*

Alongside the turmoil involved in selecting the party's presidential candidate, more political drama unfolded on the streets outside the 1968 Democratic National Convention, which was held in Chicago. All during the convention, police had been clubbing and teargassing antiwar demonstrators. During the nomination process, protesters began chanting "the whole world is watching," referring to the fact that the events were being televised. Tear gas even seeped into the twenty-fifth-floor hotel suite where Humphrey was polishing his acceptance speech.

At the Republican National Convention, the party's nominee was Richard Nixon, who had not only lost the presidency in 1960 but the California gubernatorial race two years later. Nixon claimed that the Johnson administration had failed "to use our military power effectively" or "our diplomatic power wisely" in Vietnam. He promised to "end the war and win the peace" in Southeast Asia, while curbing inflation and reestablishing law and order at home. He won the nomination by throttling the competition from his party's right wing, represented by California's Ronald Reagan (1911–), and the left wing, represented by Nelson Rockefeller.

An American soldier in
combat in Vietnam.
Reproduced by permission of
Archive Photos, Inc.

During the election, a strong third-party candidate emerged: George Wallace, now the former Alabama governor, attracted votes from the conservative wings of both parties. Between May and September, his approval ratings rose from 9 percent to 21 percent. Yet Wallace frightened many voters. He was a staunch segregationist. At his campaign stops, he seemed to incite clashes between protesters and police. His running mate, General Curtis LeMay (1906–1990), had earned notoriety for his declaration that the United States could, and probably should, "bomb the North Vietnamese back to the Stone Age."

In the end, Nixon won the presidential election of 1968 with a narrow victory: 43.4 percent of the vote. Humphrey took 42.7 percent, with Wallace earning 13.5 percent. Nixon won in thirty-two states, and his party made gains in both houses of Congress.

For More Information

BOOKS

Allen, Zita. *Black Women Leaders of the Civil Rights Movement.* Danbury, CT: Franklin Watts, 1996.

Anderson, Christopher J. *Grunts: U.S. Infantry in Vietnam.* Philadelphia: Chelsea House, 1999.

Andryszewski, Tricia. *The March on Washington, 1963: A Gathering to Be Heard.* Brookfield, CT: Millbrook Press, 1996.

Archer, Jules. *They Had a Dream: The Civil Rights Struggle from Frederick Douglas to Marcus Garvey to Martin Luther King, Jr. and Malcolm X.* New York: Viking, 1993.

Banfield, Susan. *The Fifteenth Amendment: African American Men's Right to Vote.* Springfield, NJ: Enslow Publishers, 1998.

Breitman, George, ed. *Malcolm X Speaks: Selected Speeches and Statements.* New York: Grove Press, 1990

Brubaker, Paul. *The Cuban Missile Crisis in American History.* Berkeley Heights, NJ: Enslow Publishers, 2001.

Celsi, Teresa Noel. *Jesse Jackson and Political Power.* Brookfield CT: Millbrook Press, 1991.

Cole, Michael D. *John F. Kennedy: President of the New Frontier.* Springfield, NJ: Enslow Publishers, 1996.

Darby, Jean. *Dwight D. Eisenhower: A Man Called Ike.* Minneapolis: Lerner Publications, 1989.

Darby, Jean. *Martin Luther King, Jr.* Minneapolis: Lerner Publications, 1990.

Davis, Ossie. *Just Like Martin.* New York: Simon and Schuster, 1992.

Dubovoy, Sina. *Civil Rights Leaders.* New York: Facts on File, 1997.

Edelman, Bernard, ed. *Dear America: Letters Home From Vietnam.* New York: Norton, 1985.

Evers, Myrlie. *For Us, the Living.* Jackson, MS: Banner Books, 1996.

Finkelstein, Norman H. *Thirteen Days/Ninety Miles: The Cuban Missile Crisis.* New York: J. Messner, 1994.

Goldman, Martin S. *John F. Kennedy: Portrait of a President.* New York: Facts on File, 1995.

Goldman, Martin S. *Richard M. Nixon: The Complex President.* New York: Facts on File, 1998.

Hay, Jeff, ed. *Richard Nixon.* San Diego, CA: Greenhaven Press, 2001.

Ingram, Philip. *Russia and the USSR: 1905–1991.* Cambridge, England: Cambridge University Press, 1997.

Judson, Karen. *The Presidency of the United States.* Springfield, NJ: Enslow Publishers, 1996.

Kort, Michael. *China Under Communism.* Brookfield, CT: Millbrook Press, 1994.

Kort, Michael. *The Cold War.* Brookfield, CT: Millbrook Press, 1994.

Kort, Michael. *Russia.* New York: Facts on File, 1995.

Lusane, Clarence. *No Easy Victories: Black Americans and the Vote.* New York: Franklin Watts, 1996.

Mills, Judie. *John F. Kennedy.* New York: Franklin Watts, 1988.

Mills, Judie. *Robert Kennedy.* Brookfield, CT: Millbrook Press, 1998.

Myers, Walter Dean. *Malcolm X: By Any Means Necessary.* New York: Scholastic Paperbacks, 1993.

Pietrusza, David. *John F. Kennedy.* San Diego, CA: Lucent Books, 1997.

Rasmussen, R. Kent. *Farewell Jim Crow: The Rise and Fall of Segregation in America.* New York: Facts on File, 1997.

Schraff, Anne E. *Coretta Scott King: Striving for Civil Rights.* Springfield, NJ: Enslow Publishers, 1997.

Schuman, Michael. *Lyndon B. Johnson.* Springfield, NJ: Enslow Publishers, 1998.

Schuman, Michael. *Martin Luther King, Jr.: Leader for Civil Rights.* Springfield, NJ: Enslow Publishers, 1996.

Vernell, Marjorie. *Leaders of Black Civil Rights.* San Diego, CA: Lucent Books, 2000.

Walter, Mildred Pitts. *Mississippi Challenge.* New York: Bradbury Press, 1992.

Winkler, Allan M. *The Cold War: A History in Documents.* New York: Oxford University Children's Books, 2001.

WEB SITES

The Conservative 1960s. http://www.theatlantic.com/issues/95dec/conbook/conbook.htm (accessed on August 6, 2002).

John F. Kennedy. http://www.americanpresident.org/kotrain/courses/JFK/JFK_The_American_Franchise.htm (accessed on August 6, 2002).

Lyndon B. Johnson. http://www.americanpresident.org/kotrain/courses/LBJ/LBJ_In_Brief.htm (accessed on August 6, 2002).

Peace Corps. http://www.peacecorps.gov/about/history/decades//60s.cfm (accessed on August 6, 2002).

Vietnam War and the 1960s. http://www.geocities.com/Athens/Forum/9235/vet.html (accessed on August 6, 2002).

chapter five *Lifestyles and Social Trends*

1960: Designer Pierre Cardin begins creating fashions for men, pioneering a trend away from the plain gray flannel suit.

1960: **February 1** Students stage a sit-in at a "whites-only" lunch counter in Greensboro, North Carolina.

1960: **September** "The Twist," a pop song recorded by Chubby Checker, hits the number-one spot on the *Billboard* Top 40 charts.

1961: Yo-yos become a national toy craze.

1961: Timothy Leary and Richard Alpert, Harvard psychology professors, are fired because of their experiments with hallucinogenic drugs.

1961: The President's Commission on the Status of Women is formed to study the legal and economic rights of women.

1961: **January 22–23** The National Council of Churches approves the use of birth control and family planning.

1961: **May 21–22** A bus carrying Freedom Riders is attacked by an angry mob in Montgomery, Alabama.

1962: Fashion designer Yves St. Laurent opens his own couture house.

1962: A televised tour shows First Lady Jacqueline Kennedy's redecoration of the White House, which she complet-

ed under the supervision of the National Fine Arts Commission.

1963: Vidal Sassoon creates short, geometrically inspired bob hairstyles for women.

1963: New York's Museum of Modern Art is remodeled by architect Philip Johnson.

1963: **November 22** President Kennedy is assassinated.

1964: **April 17** The Ford Motor Company unveils its new Mustang sports car.

1964: **September 28** The Warren Commission reports that Lee Harvey Oswald acted alone in killing President Kennedy.

1965: The U.S. Congress passes the Motor Vehicle Air Pollution Act.

1965: Paraphernalia, the first U.S. shop that sells "Mod" fashions exclusively, opens in New York.

1965: Toy company Wham-O introduces the Superball.

1965: **March 21** Martin Luther King Jr. leads demonstrators on a civil rights march in Selma, Alabama.

1965: **April 9** The Houston Astrodome, an enclosed air-conditioned stadium 642 feet in diameter, opens.

1966: The Black Panther Party is organized.

1966: Manufacture, distribution, or posses-sion of the hallucinogenic drug lyser-gic acid diethylamide (LSD) is made illegal.

1966: March An article in *Time* magazine warns of massive use of LSD among the young.

1966: October Betty Friedan is elected the first president of the National Organi-zation for Women (NOW).

1966: December The Diggers, a group of urban street theater actors, accuse Haight-Ashbury merchants of profiting from the then-emerging Countercul-ture and lead hundreds of costumed marchers in a Death of Money parade.

1966: December 2 U.S. Roman Catholics no longer are required to abstain from eat-ing meat on Fridays, except during Lent.

1967: Unisex clothing begins appearing in most of the major designers' fashion collections.

1967: To counter the popularity of the Ford Mustang, Chevrolet introduces the two-seat Camaro SS.

1967: The Human Be-In is held at Golden Gate Park in San Francisco, inaugu-rating the "Summer of Love."

1967: July 12–17 Race riots in Newark, New Jersey, leave twenty-six dead.

1967: July 23–30 Race riots in Detroit, Michigan, leave forty-three dead.

1968: Some established fashion couturiers offer maxi- and midi-length skirts as alternatives to the miniskirt.

1968: The Volkswagen Beetle reaches record sales of 569,292 in the United States.

1968: The 100-story John Hancock Building in Chicago becomes the world's tallest building.

1968: June 3 Artist Andy Warhol survives being shot by Valerie Solanis, a self-described feminist-revolutionary.

1968: September Feminists loudly protest against the Miss America pageant in Atlantic City, New Jersey.

1968: November 14 Yale University admits its first female students.

1969: December 6 Hell's Angels acting as security guards stab a concertgoer to death while the Rolling Stones are playing onstage at San Francisco's Altamont Music Festival.

Overview

During the 1960s, pillars of American society that had seemed so indestructible a few years before became the objects of derision. Whether they agreed or disagreed with Dwight Eisenhower, the U.S. president from 1953 through 1960, people respected him because he was the president, the commander-in-chief. Yet in the subsequent decade, two presidents, Lyndon Johnson and Richard Nixon, were openly despised and lampooned by masses of Americans because of their Vietnam War policies. A few years earlier, Americans in uniform were revered. Now, a young man returning to the United States after his mandatory service in the armed forces might be spat upon and asked to reveal the number of babies he had murdered in Vietnam. A uniformed police officer might be viewed not as a protector but as a bully who would rather harass civil rights or antiwar demonstrators than ensure their safety.

The decade was marked by violence and bloodshed. Several notable Americans, including president John F. Kennedy, U.S. Senator and presidential candidate Robert Kennedy, and civil rights leader Martin Luther King Jr., were assassinated. Civil rights workers were beaten and murdered in the South. Black schoolchildren attempting to integrate schools were met by violent mobs; blacks in several inner cities rioted during the decade; and some blacks broke from Martin Luther King Jr. and advocated violence as a means for combating racism. At the same time, individual blacks increasingly earned high-profiles in the public consciousness. They ranged from King and Black Muslim leader Malcolm X, another of the decade's assassination victims, to movie actor Sidney Poitier and television personality Bill Cosby.

As antiwar protests grew larger and more frequent, demonstrators violently clashed with police. Thousands of young people rejected the materialism of their elders and embraced what came to be known as the counterculture. They experimented with drugs, favored tie-dyed T-shirts and bellbottom jeans, and gravitated toward alternative communities. The most famous locale was the Haight-Ashbury district in San Francisco. During the second half of the decade, a women's liberation movement arose, with women organizing themselves and demanding equal rights. In the decade's final year, the gay liberation movement was born when a group of homosexual men spontaneously rioted in response to police harassment.

On an altogether different note, compact cars replaced the oversized models that had dominated the 1950s. Teens and young adults danced the Twist. Young men grew their hair long. Young women wore their skirts short. The "Mod" look revolutionized women's fashion. Under the surface was brewing the anger and violence that characterized this tumultuous American decade.

Rachel Carson (1907–1964) In 1962, marine biologist and environmentalist Rachel Carson published *The Silent Spring,* in which she warned of the hazards of environmental pollution. She spotlighted the dangers that pesticides and other toxic materials pose to plant, animal, and human life. Testifying before a U.S. Senate committee on environmental hazards in 1963, Carson argued that people should have the right to be free from poisons introduced by others into the environment. Despite attempts by the pesticide industry to discredit Carson, her views prevailed, and in 1970, the federal government formed the Environmental Protection Agency (EPA). *Photo reproduced by permission of the Corbis Corporation.*

Andre Courreges (1923–) In 1963, fashion designer Andre Courreges revolutionized the fashion world with youth-oriented designs. He spotlighted pants and short skirts, and snow-white designs. Courreges also introduced the first of what he called "space-age" designs: crisply cut clothes, featuring plenty of white, and his trademark short white boots. In 1967, he added see-through minidresses and clothing with cutout spaces that exposed women's bodies. With designer Mary Quant (1934–), Courreges is credited with creating the miniskirt. *Photo reproduced by permission of Hulton Archive.*

Betty Friedan (1921–) During the late 1960s, countless American women were trying to find more for their lives than the roles of wives and mothers could offer. They demanded equal rights and opportunities. Betty Friedan authored *The Feminine Mystique* (1963), which became one of the women's movement's bibles. In the book, she bared the falsehood of the "feminine mystique": that family and career did not mesh in women's lives. Friedan was also one of the founders of the National Organization for Women (NOW). *Photo reproduced courtesy of the Library of Congress.*

Jacqueline Bouvier Kennedy (1929–1994) Before Jacqueline Bouvier Kennedy, first ladies were viewed as matrons who quietly supported their husband's every action. Occasionally, a president's wife such as Eleanor Roosevelt (1884–1962) established her own identity as a social or political advocate. However, the wife of President John F. Kennedy (1917–1963) was a new kind of first lady. Jackie was young. She was stylish. She was elegant. She became a model of style for millions of American women. *Photo reproduced by permission of Hulton Archive.*

Timothy Leary (1920–1996) Timothy Leary, at one time a lecturer in psychology at Harvard, became one of the gurus of the hippie/drug culture when he urged America's young to "turn on, tune in, drop out." In particular, Leary encouraged the use of the hallucinogenic drug lysergic acid diethylamide (LSD). As the U.S. government stepped up enforcement of drug possession laws, Leary spent the late 1960s and beyond evading jail. After eventually serving various prison terms, Leary became a social commentator and lecturer. *Photo reproduced by permission of Archive Photos, Inc.*

Malcolm X (1919–1965) Malcolm X was a prominent figure in the Civil Rights movement of the early- and mid-1960s. A member of the Nation of Islam, often called the Black Muslims, Malcolm encouraged his followers to follow militant racial separatism instead of the nonviolent tactics and integrationist demands of fellow civil rights activist Martin Luther King Jr. As Malcolm continued to become more popular with the people, the inner circle of the Nation of Islam became jealous and suspended Malcolm in 1963. Malcolm was then assassinated by three Black Muslims in 1965 while giving a speech in New York. *Photo reproduced by permission of AP/Wide World Photos.*

Benjamin Spock (1903–1998) During the 1950s and the 1960s, American mothers regularly consulted the *Common Sense Book of Baby and Child Care* (1946) by Benjamin Spock. He also was one of America's most prominent voices of protest against the war in Vietnam. In 1968, Spock was put on trial for allegedly attempting to hinder the military draft. While on the witness stand, he asked, "What is the use of physicians like myself trying to help parents bring up children, healthy and happy, to have them killed in such numbers for a cause that is ignoble?" *Photo reproduced courtesy of the Library of Congress.*

Robert Venturi (1925–) In 1966 Robert Venturi created controversy with the publication of *Complexity and Contradiction in Architecture,* in which he lambasted the reigning giants of architecture. Venturi argued for architecture that spotlighted creativity and variation. Modernists rejected older forms and ornamentation; to Venturi's way of thinking, it was entirely appropriate to incorporate these forms (which included everything from wall ornamentation to Roman arches and Corinthian columns) in contemporary design. Venturi's unorthodox approach placed him at the forefront of postmodern architecture. *Photo reproduced by permission of AP/Wide World Photos.*

◆◇ *Topics in the News* . . . .

❖ ASSASSINATION, PROTEST, AND VIOLENCE

Of all the domestic upheaval that captured headlines during the 1960s, none was more shocking than the assassination of President John F. Kennedy (1917–1963). After the grandfatherly presence in the White House of Republican Dwight Eisenhower (1890–1969), Kennedy, a Democrat, brought youth and spirit to national politics. He was a young man, in his early forties, when he won election in 1960. His wife Jacqueline (1929–1994) was stylish and attractive. Kennedy was also the father of young children. His daughter Caroline (1957–), was three years old when he was elected. His son John Jr. (1960–1999), popularly known as John-John, was just a couple of days short of his third birthday when Kennedy was murdered while parading in a motorcade past the Texas School Book Depository in downtown Dallas. The date, November 22, 1963, instantly became a landmark in American history.

People around the world reacted with a special horror at the news of Kennedy's death. Not only was he youthful and vital, but Americans in particular had come to believe that such acts only occurred elsewhere, in less-civilized countries. Kennedy's assailant was Lee Harvey Oswald (1939–1963), a Depository employee and former U.S. Marine sharpshooter. Oswald had a murky past. He had defected to the Soviet Union, where he lived between 1959 and 1962. Then he returned to the United States, where he became involved in pro-Cuba activities.

In the hours and days following the assassination, life in the United States came to a standstill. Americans watched their television sets in disbelief as a caisson, a horse-drawn wheeled vehicle containing the slain president's casket, rolled down Pennsylvania Avenue in Washington, D.C. Following the caisson was a riderless horse. In an image etched in the memories of those who witnessed it, Kennedy's little son John saluted as the caisson passed by.

Kennedy was not the only national leader to be cut down by assassination during the decade. Martin Luther King Jr. (1929–1968), the civil rights leader who advocated nonviolence as a means of protesting racism, was felled by a bullet in April 1968. Two months later, Robert Kennedy (1925–1968) was also murdered. Kennedy was the slain president's younger brother and a leading contender that year for the Democratic Party's presidential nomination.

Assassinations of public figures covered a wide political spectrum. In 1965, controversial Black Muslim leader Malcolm X (1925–1965) was

Racial conflicts eventually led to destructive riots in major U.S. cities, such as Los Angeles and Detroit.
Reproduced by permission of AP/Wide World Photos.

shot to death. Two years later, George Lincoln Rockwell (1918–1967), head of the American Nazi Party, was murdered.

Throughout the decade, the then-burgeoning Civil Rights movement was met with a violent response by white supremacists. Civil rights activist Medgar Evers (1925–1963) was killed in June 1963. Evers had, in 1954, become the first Mississippi field secretary of the National Organization for the Advancement of Colored People (NAACP). The accused killer, Byron De La Beckwith (1920–2001), stood trial twice during the 1960s, but all-white juries failed to reach verdicts. In 1994, De La Beckwith, a decorated World War II veteran and retired fertilizer salesman, was retried and convicted. He was sentenced to life in prison.

There were many other victims of racist violence. Bostonian James Reeb (1927–1965), a Unitarian minister, died following a beating while in Selma, Alabama, where he went to assist in a voting rights drive. Three civil rights workers affiliated with the Congress of Racial Equality (CORE)—Michael Schwerner (1939–1964), James Chaney (1943–1964), and Andrew Goodman (1943–1964)—were murdered in Mississippi. Viola Liuzzo (1925–1965), a Detroit housewife helping with voter registration, was killed in Alabama.

Violence occurred against groups of people, as well as against individuals. In the early 1960s, the Freedom Riders were a target. The Freedom Riders were a group of blacks and whites of both sexes and all ages who came to the South to test Supreme Court desegregation rulings and similar federal legislation. They rode from town to town on a bus, often with whites at the back and blacks at the front, and they sat together at "white" and "colored"-only lunch counters. Often, they faced angry mobs and their buses were firebombed. Four young girls, ages eleven to fourteen, were killed when their Birmingham, Alabama, church was bombed in September 1963. Police dogs and high-pressure fire hoses were used against schoolchildren attempting to enroll in previously segregated schools.

Much violence of the era focused on the desegregation of educational institutions. In 1962, a court order directed that James Meredith (1933–), a black man, be allowed to enroll at the University of Mississippi. A mob attacked the federal marshals who had been sent to enforce the ruling. President Kennedy ordered 5,000 army and National Guard troops onto the "Ole Miss" campus to halt the rioting. Casualties included 166 injured marshals, 28 by gunshot wounds; 40 injured soldiers and guardsman; and two dead civilians, one a French journalist.

Promoters of voter rights were also targets. Only 3 percent of eligible blacks in Selma, Alabama, were registered to vote in the mid-1960s. On the second day of a 1965 voter registration campaign, sixty-seven blacks were arrested. Hundreds more followed. The Selma police employed violent methods to turn back protesters, who at one point were chased with electric cattle prods. An Alabama state trooper shot a demonstrator, who subsequently died. In one famous confrontation, demonstrators attempting to march from Selma to the state capital of Montgomery were attacked by club and tear gas-wielding state troopers. When the marchers retreated, they were attacked by the Selma police.

In the northern and western United States, riots flared in the black neighborhoods of major American cities, mostly during what came to be known as "long, hot summers." In 1964, disturbances broke out in New

York's Harlem community, and in Brooklyn's Brownsville neighborhood. The following year, in the Watts area of Los Angeles, rioting resulted in thirty deaths. The California National Guard was called in to restore order. In 1966, more than forty similar outbreaks occurred across the nation. More than 160 followed in 1967. Nationwide disturbances also broke out in the aftermath of the Martin Luther King Jr. assassination in 1968.

Violent confrontation escalated during the summer of 1968 on the streets of Chicago, the site of the Democratic National Convention. In what an official government report dubbed a "police riot," Chicago policemen beat thousands of protestors. Many anti-Vietnam war demonstrations, which were by then quite frequent on college campuses, ended in bloody showdowns between police and protesters. Over a thousand were injured and seven hundred were arrested in October 1967, when troops used rifle butts to prevent demonstrators from entering the Pentagon. Meanwhile, such fringe groups as the Weathermen and the Black Panther Party made headlines with violent activity on behalf of their causes. The Weathermen were determined to "bring the (Vietnam) war home" by instigating violent action. The Black Panthers, who took the position that they were at war with America's white power structure, engaged in several bloody shoot-outs with police.

Gays also were becoming increasingly politicized and inclined to engage in civil disobedience on behalf of their cause. In June 1969,

Protestors demonstrated their desire for peace and an end to the Vietnam War. **Reproduced by permission of the Corbis Corporation.**

patrons of Stonewall, a gay men's bar in New York's Greenwich Village, refused to silently comply with police during a routine raid. Instead, they fought back. A riot ensued, and the bar was set on fire. This has been called the start of the gay rights movement.

In total, all these incidents were evidence of a growing trend in American society to use violence as a means of expressing one's point of view.

❖ THE WARREN COMMISSION AND ITS CRITICS

Immediately in its aftermath, the American people demanded to know the facts behind the assassination of John F. Kennedy. Was Lee Harvey Oswald the lone gunman? Were other conspirators with him that day in Dallas? Had he concocted his deadly scheme alone, or did any one of a number of Kennedy's political foes back him?

Oswald would not live to answer these or other questions. Two days after the assassination, he was shot dead while being transferred from the Dallas city jail to the county lockup. His assailant was Jack Ruby (1911–1967), a Dallas nightclub owner.

To determine the facts surrounding the assassination, Lyndon Johnson (1908–1973), Kennedy's successor, appointed a bipartisan investigative committee. It was headed by U.S. Supreme Court Chief Justice Earl Warren (1891–1974) and became known as the Warren Commission. In September 1964, the commission issued an 888-page report in which it concluded that Oswald had acted alone.

While most people accept the findings of the Warren Commission, decades later there are still those who fault the commission's findings. Critics cite inconsistencies in witnesses' testimony and suggest that the images on a 26-second-long, 8mm film of the Kennedy motorcade, shot by Dallas dress manufacturer Abraham Zapruder (1905–1970), do not correspond to the taped sound of the gunshots.

❖ THE ASSASSINATION OF MALCOLM X

Malcolm X (1925–1965) was born Malcolm Little, and his early life was marred by tragedy. His father, a Baptist preacher who embraced the teachings of Black Nationalist leader Marcus Garvey (1887–1940), was murdered in 1931 by the Black Legion, a Ku Klux Klan-like racist group. Despite the mutilated condition of his body, the death was officially ruled a suicide.

By the time he reached manhood, Little had drifted into a criminal lifestyle. In 1946, he was sentenced to prison for armed robbery. While in jail, he became self-educated, in part through reading and copying the entire dictionary. He joined the Nation of Islam (Black Muslims), a religious sect that emphasizes self-discipline and preaches the superiority of the black race. He changed his name to Malcolm X and, after his release from prison, evolved into one of the sect's most forceful speakers. Unlike civil rights leaders such as Martin Luther King Jr. (1920–1968), who advocated nonviolence, Malcolm declared that blacks should employ "any means necessary," including violence, to win their liberty.

Even within the Black Muslim movement, Malcolm was a controversial figure. He clashed with Elijah Muhammad (1897–1975), the movement's leader; Malcolm questioned Elijah's sincerity, while Elijah reportedly had become jealous of Malcolm's rising popularity. After being suspended from the Muslims, Malcolm traveled to Mecca and embraced orthodox Islam. When he returned to the United States in 1964, he put forth a more conciliatory tone with regard to race relations. He no longer was a black separatist and even admitted that not all whites were racists.

While speaking in a ballroom in New York's Harlem district in 1965, Malcolm X was assassinated by three Black Muslim followers.

❖ BLACK AMERICA ON SCREEN

Through the late 1940s, many Hollywood studio films depicted African Americans with simple, degrading stereotypes: Comical menials who were servile and stupid and who butchered the English language. Black actors were character actors and played only supporting roles.

By mid-century, the portrayal of black characters began to change. A cycle of films indicted stereotyping and discrimination and pleaded for racial tolerance. Four early films with this tone were released in 1949: *Intruder in the Dust; Pinky; Lost Boundaries;* and *Home of the Brave.* All featured three-dimensional black characters who were victims of a prejudicial society, each suffering solely because of their skin color.

With the mushrooming Civil Rights movement in the 1950s and 1960s came the first black Hollywood star, Sidney Poitier (1924–), who debuted in *No Way Out* (1950), playing a young doctor. Poitier was good-looking and charming. He became the first black star to win a Best Actor Academy Award for his performance as a wandering ex-GI who helps a band of nuns build a chapel in *Lilies of the Field* (1963). Among his most consequential films are *The Defiant Ones* (1958), about black and white escaped convicts who are chained to each other and whose mutual dislike turns to respect; *In the Heat of the Night* (1967), in which a pair of adversaries, a black Philadelphia cop and a white small-town Southern sheriff, work together on a murder investigation; and *Guess Who's Coming to Din-*

ner (1967), spotlighting an interracial romance between a black intellectual and a young Caucasian woman.

During the 1960s, several independent films produced outside the
Hollywood studios offered uncommonly vivid slices of African American
life. The characters in *One Potato Two Potato* (1964), a frank study of an
interracial marriage, were more realistic than those in *Guess Who's Coming
to Dinner.* *Nothing But a Man* (1964), the story of a black railroad worker
dealing with a combination of racial prejudice and self-denial, is extraor-
dinary if only because it portrays a black character as he exists within his
own culture.

On television, African American entertainers had long appeared as
guest stars, most notably dancing and singing on variety shows. Nat King
Cole (1919–1965), a popular jazz musician-singer, had his own short-lived
variety series, *The Nat King Cole Show* (1956–57). However, the first black
character on a major primetime dramatic TV series appeared in the 1960s.
The show was *I Spy* (1965–68), and it chronicled the exploits of a two
secret agents, one white and the other black. This character, Alexander
Scott, was played by Bill Cosby (1937–), who was then primarily known as
a stand-up comic. In future decades, Cosby would become one of the most
successful and powerful television personalities in the United States.

❖ CARS

During the 1960s, Americans by the millions traded in their oversized,
gas-guzzling cars for more compact foreign and American-made models.
These cars were more practical because they were easier to park and less
expensive to drive. They also were sportier and more high-performance
than the traditional mid-century family vehicle.

Many enthusiasts rate the Ford Mustang as the quintessential 1960s
automobile. The original Mustang hit the marketplace in 1964. Its cre-
ators wanted it to be low-priced (at approximately $2,500), sporty enough
to appeal to the youth market, and available with a diverse assortment of
options.

The original Mustang was neither the fastest nor the most powerful
car available. Yet it became an instant hit. In 1966, more than 541,000
units were sold, accounting for 6 percent of all U.S. car sales.

❖ COUNTERCULTURE

Life in American suburbia during the 1950s is often described as
orderly and convenient, and at worst, sterile. The media image was of

happy, contented families; in reality, the pursuit of the suburban dream life often produced stressed-out husbands and fathers, bored and tired wives and mothers, and children who rejected their parent's lifestyles and values. As American children grew to maturity in the 1960s, many created their own counterculture: a world all their own, the foundation of which consisted of great quantities of "sex, drugs, and rock 'n' roll."

Those in the counterculture claimed to be nonmaterialistic. To show this, many preferred to wear faded, ripped blue jeans rather than crisp new ones. Peace, love, and marijuana were preferred over war, aggression, and martinis. Love was "free," or not restricted to monogamous relationships. Drugs users marveled at how drugs, especially hallucinogens, could "expand" their minds. Those young people who fully denounced materialism, dropped out of the mainstream, and embraced counterculture values were known as hippies. To their elders, and to those among their peers who continued to embrace more traditional values, hippies seemed irresponsible and foolish.

Counterculture communities emerged across the United States. The two most famous were on the West Coast, in the Haight-Ashbury section of San Francisco, and on the East Coast, in New York's East Village. Between 1966 and 1967, young people flocked by the thousands to such communities. They readily abandoned the physical comfort of their parents' suburban homes for the adventure and uncertainty of day-to-day living in communities like "the Haight" or "the Village." By mid-1967, tens of thousands of teens and "twenty-somethings" had descended on San Francisco in search of the free love, antiestablishment, drug-soaked utopia they thought they would find there. That summer was dubbed the first "Summer of Love." Although that title has also been attributed to the one that followed, by the summer of 1968, the hippie movement had overlapped more fully with the angry protests of the antiwar and civil rights movements. The idealism of those who believed The Beatles when they sang "All You Need is Love" began to disintegrate into disillusionment.

Even before the "Summer of Love" had ended, reports of drug-related murders and other less violent crimes in counterculture communities were harsh evidence of the naiveté of those who felt that "good vibrations" could remake the world. As evidenced by reports of tainted drugs and subsequent "bad trips," the use of hallucinogens like lysergic acid diethylamide (LSD) did not always result in pleasant journeys. Furthermore, there was no economic foundation on which the counterculture could endure. How long would rock bands perform for free in parks when they could earn millions by selling tickets in concert halls?

While fragments of the counterculture survived into the 1970s, parents and conservatives never quite understood or approved of it. In the late 1960s, many young people adopted as their motto a phrase that reverberated through the era: "Never trust anyone over thirty." Indeed, it often seemed as if older and younger adults resided on different planets.

❖ FADS

The 1960s was a decade in which Americans embraced a range of fads. Children played with yo-yos and Superballs (tiny rubber balls that would bounce for a full minute when dropped). Teens danced the Twist, first popularized in 1960 by singer Chubby Checker (1941–). The dance became so trendy that First Lady Jacqueline Kennedy (1929–1994) even threw a Twist party at the White House! Other dance crazes followed, including the Watusi, Frug, Pony, Swim, Mashed Potato, and Jerk.

Before the antiwar movement engulfed campuses, college students engaged in piano-wrecking, kissathons, and telephone talkathons. The Beatles, those mop-topped lads from Liverpool, not only defined the spirit of 1960s youth but provided the basis for a whole industry of Beatles boots, wigs, wallets, games, and movies. Surfing became a fad, spurred on by the "California sounds" of rock groups such as The Beach Boys and Jan and Dean. Teens flocked to theaters to see such silly but popular "beach" movies as *Beach Party, Beach Blanket Bingo, Bikini Beach, Muscle Beach Party, Dr. Goldfoot and the Bikini Machine,* and *How to Stuff a Wild Bikini,* which all starred Frankie Avalon (1940–) and Annette Funicello (1942–).

❖ FASHION

On the 1960s fashion front, women increasingly rejected dresses and skirts in favor of pants and pantsuits. The "masculinity" of women wearing pants was tempered by gloves, jewelry, and dressy handbags and patent leather shoes. From about 1963 on, hemlines crept higher and higher. Many younger women favored miniskirts (scandalously short skirts), and microminis (which just barely, but not always, hid undergarments).

The overall look in women's fashions, especially during the early years of the decade, emphasized a combination of simplicity and ladylike elegance. Solid colors were preferred over patterns. The invention of pantyhose freed women from the burdens of girdles, garter belts, and other traditional undergarments. Early in the decade, women wore their hair in full, oversized "beehives" or more moderate bouffant styles. Around the mid-1960s, younger women rejected the bouffant and beehive for longer, more "natural" styles. In order to achieve these so-called natural styles, many girls set their hair using orange-juice-can rollers, and some even ironed their hair to achieve an ultra-straight look!

*The minidress was a new
clothing item that gained
popularity because of its
scandalously short
length.* **Reproduced by
permission of the
Corbis Corporation.**

*Unisex clothing became
increasingly popular
during the 1960s.*

During the decade, men became more fashion-conscious. Where the conservative gray flannel suit had once been the rule for businessmen, by the mid-1960s a wide range of styles became popular, with European designers marketing suits with much slimmer lines. Ties and belts became narrower. More adventurous men wore suits in brighter colors. Instead of keeping their hair short and neatly trimmed, males of all generations generally wore their hair longer. Some even began visiting unisex hairstyling salons, shops that catered to both men and women, rather than barber shops.

During the second half of the 1960s, millions of young men let their hair grow to lengths that rivaled that of their sisters or girlfriends. At the time, extra-long, unkempt hair on males was not so much a fashion style as a political statement, particularly against the war in Vietnam. Meanwhile, blacks of both sexes wore full, natural Afro cuts.

In the early 1960s, teen girls wore sweater/blouse/skirt combinations. Among the popular styles were woolen A-line or pleated skirts; cardigan sweaters; and solid-colored or subdued flowery-print cotton blouses with button-down or Bermuda collars. Outfits were completed by Bass Weejuns slip-on loafers and flesh-colored stockings or knee-high socks. Some younger women preferred one-piece dresses, occasionally worn with a belt at the waist; however, completely waist-less dresses, known as shifts, were also worn, both in and out of school. Girls also increasingly wore pants in general and blue jeans in particular. Some outfits, such as matching jeans and denim jackets, were marketed for both sexes ("unisex").

As in previous decades, boys and girls were required to dress formally while in school throughout most of the 1960s; dress codes didn't change significantly until the 1970s. Acceptable school clothes for girls included dresses or skirts and blouses—pants of any kind were taboo—while boys donned button-down shirts, twill and khaki-type trousers, and, in some schools, even sports jackets and ties. As the decade moved forward and young people attempted to find ways to separate themselves from their elders, they embraced what might be described as "anti-fashion." Members of both sexes rejected established fashion of any kind in favor of nontraditional looks. They wore their own unorthodox uniforms: pea coats, faded bell-bottom jeans, and T-shirts that were tie-dyed in bright spirals and circles. Second-hand clothing stores and army-navy surplus stores became popular venues for adding to one's wardrobe. Sandals became the favored type of footwear, but going barefoot was preferred. Many younger women wore little if any makeup. Going braless also became a standard practice.

❖ FASHION: "MOD"

In the 1960s, the "Mod" (or "Chelsea") look revolutionized clothing styles for the young and helped create a new phenomenon: a youth fashion market.

Previously, major designers targeted adults. Now, however, teenagers had more money in their pockets than in previous generations, and girls in particular wanted to spend these dollars on clothes that were tailored specifically for them. During the 1950s, Mary Quant (1934–), a British milliner's shop employee, opened Bazaar, a clothing shop on King's Row in the Chelsea section of London, England. Quant believed that clothes for youth should reflect youthfulness and should be spirited and unconventional rather than stuffy and boring. Her idea was to create clothing that could be worn and then disposed of when new styles and trends emerged. So she filled Bazaar with clothes that she personally designed and that had a fresh new feel: simple, short dresses in black or with wild geometric patterns and strong colors; knee-length jumpers; and balloon-style dresses. Quant kept adding designs and styles, and her store became phenomenally successful. Not only did Bazaar draw the young and trendy, but it influenced clothing styles for young people on both sides of the Atlantic Ocean. Eventually, Quant supplied clothing to 150 shops in Great Britain and 320 in the United States.

Bazaar also was hailed as the first fashion boutique: A relaxed, nonpressured environment in which shoppers could browse the racks while listening to popular music playing in the background. Almost single-handedly, Quant made London the 1960s fashion capital of the world.

*Demonstrators from the
National Women's
Liberation Movement
were antifashion and
rebelled against trends
and society by wearing
second-hand clothing.*
**Reproduced by permission of
the Corbis Corporation.**

❖ FOLK REVIVAL

During the early 1960s, folk music, (music made and handed down among the common people) enjoyed a burst of popularity. It was the

Twiggy (1949–), who in the late 1960s was the world's most famous fashion model, became the embodiment of "Mod." Unlike females who were admired for their fuller figures and long, luxurious hair, Twiggy was slender and boyish, with a close-cropped Vidal Sassoon haircut. She became a trendsetter in the fashion world.

Another fashion style also emerged in London that became popular in the United States: the Carnaby Street look. Long, straight-cut dresses patterned with combinations of stripes and dots were a Carnaby Street trademark.

music of choice for thinking individuals, many of them college students, who were bothered by what they felt was the inanity of rock and roll and distressed by the specter of nuclear holocaust, racial disharmony, and other societal ills.

Bob Dylan, Joan Baez, Pete Seeger, Ramblin' Jack Elliot, Tom Paxton, Judy Collins, Joni Mitchell, Phil Ochs, and Peter, Paul and Mary were a few of the era's top folk performers. Two compositions by Dylan (1941–) mirrored issues of primary concern to folk aficionados: "Blowin' in the Wind," an appeal for racial harmony that was a hit for Peter, Paul, and Mary; and "The Times They Are A-Changin'," which foresaw a future in which the emerging generation would add a much-needed dose of humanism to the social order.

In 1965, Dylan abandoned the acoustic guitar, the instrument of choice for folk singers. First he recorded "Subterranean Homesick Blues" with electric instruments and then appeared with an electric guitar at the Newport Folk Festival. The folk purists booed Dylan off the Newport stage, but he had transformed himself into a rock star, and his acoustic-to-electric conversion signaled the beginning of the end of the folk music revival.

❖ GOVERNMENT FUNDING OF THE ARTS

During the 1960s, the U.S. government became increasingly arts-oriented. In 1964, through the U.S. Information Agency, it first supported American entries at the Venice Biennale art exhibition. In 1965, President Lyndon Johnson (1908–1973) signed into the law the Federal Aid to the Arts Bill, which created the National Endowment for the Arts (NEA) and

The Black Arts Movement

The 1960s saw a generation of African American playwrights, novelists, essayists, poets, and critics arriving at the forefront of American arts and letters. Their voices, always clear and loud and often radical, paralleled the escalating Civil Rights movement.

Among them were Amiri Baraka (formerly known as LeRoi Jones), Larry Neal, Addison Gayle Jr., Hoyt Fuller, and Nikki Giovanni. In their writings, they noted that blacks and whites lived in separate cultures and thus should have separate arts.

the National Endowment for the Humanities (NEH). These and similar organizations directly funneled financial support to individual artists. In 1966, modern-dance choreographers Merce Cunningham, Alvin Ailey, Paul Taylor, and Alwin Nikolais each received $5,000, while choreographer Martha Graham secured $40,000 to produce two new works and $141,000 to mount a national tour of her company.

Public funding of the arts provoked arguments from all sides of the political spectrum. Some government officials and taxpayers felt that, if they were paying for art, they had the right to control its content. As a result, government-subsidized art that was perceived by some to be controversial because it challenged conventional views became the center of a political firestorm, with conservatives damning the artists and arts-funders and liberals defending the rights of artists to enjoy freedom of expression.

On the other hand, arts funding allowed for an increased public appreciation of the relevance of the arts to everyday life. This awareness came in many forms: the presence of paintings and sculpture in public places; a rise in the number of museums on college campuses; an increase in the number of regional theaters; and the establishment of public radio and television stations, which offered audiences noncommercial cultural and educational programming.

❖ TRYING THE CHICAGO SEVEN

In the aftermath of a bloody August 1968 confrontation between police and antiwar demonstrators outside the Democratic National Convention in

Chicago, several protesters were indicted and charged with inciting a riot. The defendants were David Dellinger, Rennie Davis, Tom Hayden, Jerry Rubin, Abbie Hoffman, John Froines, Lee Weiner, and Bobby Seale.

Their pretrial strategy was to treat the case as political theater. They were determined to disrupt the proceedings, so that no conviction could be obtained that would stand on appeal. Among their rationales: Even though many believed that the police were the instigators of the violence, none of Chicago's finest had been indicted; and the trial would allow the defendants the opportunity to publicize their views. Further heightening the proceeding's confrontational nature was its judge: seventy-four-year-old Julius Hoffman (c. 1896–1983), who was not known for his patience. As the trial began, Judge Hoffman attempted to jail four lawyers for contempt because they had withdrawn from the case. Then he refused to allow defense lawyers to question prospective jurors about their attitudes toward youth culture and the Vietnam War. The trial itself was no less stormy; at one point, Judge Hoffman ordered Seale, national chairman of the Black Panther Party, bound and gagged.

In the end, Froines and Weiner were acquitted of all charges, while the others were convicted under the Anti-Riot Act of 1968, which prohibited traveling across state lines with the intention of inciting a riot. While the jury deliberated their fates, Judge Hoffman sentenced them and two of their attorneys to jail terms for contempt of court. A U.S. Court of Appeals eventually overturned all convictions and sentences, ruling that the judge failed to allow defense attorneys to properly question jurors and neglected to let key defense witnesses testify.

Several of those cited for contempt were retried on those charges and were found guilty. However, the presiding judge decided not to sentence them to any jail time.

For More Information

BOOKS

Andryszewski, Tricia. *Gay Rights*. Brookfield, CT: Twenty-First Century Books, 2000.

Bergman, Carol. *Sidney Poitier*. New York: Chelsea House, 1989.

Bode, Janet. *The Colors of Freedom: Immigrant Stories*. New York: Franklin Watts, 1999.

Breitman, George, ed. *Malcolm X Speaks: Selected Speeches and Statements*. New York: Grove Press, 1990.

Chafe, William H. *The Road to Equality: American Women Since 1962.* New York: Oxford University Press, 1994.

Cole, Michael D. *John F. Kennedy: President of the New Frontier.* Springfield, NJ: Enslow Publishers, 1996.

Darby, Jean. *Martin Luther King, Jr.* Minneapolis: Lerner Publications, 1990.

Davis, Ossie. *Just Like Martin.* New York: Simon & Schuster, 1992.

Evers, Myrlie. *For Us, the Living.* Jackson, MS: Banner Books, 1996.

Faber, Doris. *The Smithsonian Book of First Ladies: Their Lives, Times, and Issues.* New York: Henry Holt & Company, 1996.

Feinberg, Barbara Silberdick. *America's First Ladies: Changing Expectations.* New York: Franklin Watts, 1998.

Galas, Judith. *Gay Rights.* San Diego, CA: Lucent Books, 1995.

Goldman, Martin S. *John F. Kennedy: Portrait of a President.* New York: Facts on File, 1995.

Greenberg, Cara. *Up to Pop: Furniture in the 1960s.* Boston: Little, Brown & Company, 1999.

Guernsey, Joann Bren. *Voices of Feminism: Past, Present, and Future.* Minneapolis: Lerner Publications, 1996.

Hampton, Wilborn. *Kennedy Assassinated! The World Mourns: A Reporter's Story.* Cambridge, MA: Candlewick Press, 1997.

Henricksson, John. *Rachel Carson: The Environmental Movement.* Brookfield, CT: Millbrook Press, 1991.

Hurley, Jennifer A., ed. *Feminism: Opposing Viewpoints.* San Diego, CA: Greenhaven Press, 2000.

Jezer, Marty. *Rachel Carson.* New York: Chelsea House, 1988.

Kallen, Stuart A., ed. *Sixties Counterculture.* San Diego, CA: Greenhaven Press, 2000.

Landau, Elaine. *John F. Kennedy, Jr.* Brookfield, CT: Twenty-First Century Books, 2000.

Mills, Judie. *John F. Kennedy.* New York: Franklin Watts, 1988.

Mills, Judie. *Robert Kennedy.* Brookfield, CT: Millbrook Press, 1998.

Myers, Walter Dean. *Malcolm X: By Any Means Necessary.* New York: Scholastic Paperbacks, 1993.

Olian, JoAnne, editor. *Everyday Fashions of the Sixties, as Pictured in Sears Catalogs.* Mineola, NY: Dover Publications, 1999.

Oliver, Marilyn Tower. *Gay and Lesbian Rights: A Struggle.* Springfield, NJ: Enslow Publications, 1998.

Pietrusza, David. *John F. Kennedy.* San Diego, CA: Lucent Books, 1997.

Powe-Temperley, Kitty. *The 60s: Mods & Hippies.* Milwaukee: Gareth Stevens, 2000.

Roleff, Tamara, ed. *Gay Rights.* San Diego, CA: Greenhaven Press, 1996.

Schuman, Michael. *Bill Cosby: Actor and Comedian.* Springfield, NJ: Enslow Publishers, 1995.

Schuman, Michael. *Martin Luther King, Jr.: Leader for Civil Rights.* Springfield, NJ: Enslow Publishers, 1996.

Schwager, Tina, and Michele Schuerger. *Gutsy Girls: Young Women Who Dare.* Minneapolis: Free Spirit Publishing, 1999.

Siegel, Beatrice. *Murder on the Highway: The Viola Liuzzo Story.* New York: Four Winds Press, 1993.

Silver, Diane. *The New Civil War: The Lesbian and Gay Struggle for Civil Rights.* New York: Franklin Watts, 1997.

Southard, Andy. *Hot Rods and Custom Cars of the 1960s.* Osceola, WI: Motorbooks International, 1997.

Strong, Susan. *The Greatness of Girls: Famous Women Talk About Growing Up.* Kansas City, MO: Andrews McMeel, 2001.

WEB SITES

Fashion Flashbacks. http://www.fashion-flashbacks.com/20cen/20cen1960s.html (accessed on August 6, 2002).

1960s Flashback—Potpourri. http://www.1960sflashback.com/1960/Potpourri.asp (accessed on August 6, 2002).

Top Ten: Fads. http://www.mpimedia.com/wpa/tank/topten/fads/fads.html (accessed on August 6, 2002).

The Tumultuous 1960s. http://home.earthlink.net/~gfeldmeth/lec.1960.html (accessed on August 6, 2002).

Women in Folk Music—Female Singers and Songwriters. http://womenshistory.about.com/cs/musicfolk/ (accessed on August 6, 2002).

chapter six **Medicine and Health**

1960: An orally administered polio vaccine, developed by Albert Sabin, is introduced in the United States.

1960: April A breast implant is constructed from silicone gel.

1960: May Birth control pills are approved for widespread use in the United States.

1960: December In order to practice in the United States, foreign-trained doctors are required to pass special tests.

1961: April An epidemic of sexually transmitted diseases, such as syphilis and gonorrhea, is reported among American teenagers.

1961: May Blood from a cadaver (dead body) is used to give a transfusion.

1962: Radiation, chemotherapy, and steroids are used to fight leukemia.

1962: June A severed arm is successfully reattached to a twelve-year-old boy.

1962: June Various government proposals for offering America's elderly adequate health insurance are considered.

1962: December The first human kidney transplant using a nonrelative as a donor is completed.

1963: A measles vaccine is made available.

1963: Valium, an antianxiety, anticonvulsant drug, is introduced.

1963: May The first human liver transplant is performed.

1963: June The first human lung transplant is performed.

1963: June 8 The American Heart Association announces an antismoking campaign.

1964: Approximately one million abortions are performed annually in the United States. Most are illegal.

1964: A rubella (German measles) epidemic sweeps the country.

1964: April The one-hundred-billionth Bayer aspirin tablet is produced.

1964: June 24 The Federal Trade Commission (FTC) proclaims that, beginning in 1965, cigarette packaging must feature health warnings.

1965: The female hormone estrogen is found to prevent osteoporosis (bone degeneration).

1965: Soft contact lenses are invented.

1965: March The New York Blood Center, a computerized blood bank, opens in New York City.

1965: May A condition called "surfer's knee" is described as being a result of frequent kneeling on surfboards.

1966: January 1 Tobacco companies must print the words "Caution: Cigarette smoking may be hazardous to your health" on cigarette packaging.

1966: March An epidemic of thyroid disease in children is reported in St. George, Utah, located downwind from a Nevada nuclear test site.

1966: March A stapling device that rapidly closes incisions during surgery is marketed.

1966: July 1 The Medicare health insurance plan for Americans over sixty-five years old is instituted.

1967: Authorities in Evanston, Illinois, report that, during a twenty-year period, fluoridated water has reduced residents' cavities by 58 percent.

1967: Doctors at Chicago's Cook County Hospital hook up a cystoscope (which looks into the bladder) to a color television and videotape machine.

1967: For the first year since records on the disease were initiated, no American dies of rabies.

1967: May Colorado becomes the first state to liberalize abortion laws.

1967: December Christiaan Barnard performs the first human-to-human heart transplant operation.

1968: A meningitis vaccine is developed and tested on military recruits.

1968: January The U.S. Public Health Service reports that malnutrition among America's poor is just as severe as in developing countries.

1968: March A kidney-storage unit that can save donor kidneys awaiting transplant for up to three days becomes available.

1969: Many hysterectomies, particularly in women under forty, are reported to be often unnecessary.

1969: The Medical Information Telephone System (MIST), a consultation service for doctors, is started.

1969: A new incubator for premature babies is developed.

1969: April 4 Denton Cooley performs the first complete artificial heart transplant.

1969: October 18 The Department of Health, Education, and Welfare bans cyclamates (artificial sweeteners), which cause cancer and birth defects.

1969: November 20 Because of its health and environmental hazards, the Department of Agriculture announces plans to phase out use of the pesticide DDT (dichlorodiphenyltrichloroethane).

Overview

Great advances were made during the 1960s in the areas of medicine and health care. Viruses were isolated, and vaccines to combat a host of diseases, from measles to meningitis, became available. A range of products and procedures were developed or newly marketed. Among them were breast implants; soft contact lenses; home kidney dialysis machines (which remove poisons from the blood of patients suffering from kidney failure); cryosurgery (surgery by freezing); oral birth control pills and intrauterine devices, also known as IUDs (which allow women control over their bodies' reproductive cycle); fertility drugs and artificial insemination (which allow childless couples to become parents); and Valium (a drug that battles anxiety). Limb reattachments and liver, lung, and heart transplant operations were completed successfully. Efforts were made to develop an artificial heart that could be used during surgery. Coronary artery bypass surgery was also initiated. Patients may have lamented that fewer doctors packed up their medical bags and visited them in their homes when they were ill. However, the development of new machines and drugs that allowed physicians to more accurately treat illnesses made visits to the doctor's office far more practical from the standpoint of detecting and curing disease.

While the research and development of wonder drugs alleviated, and in some cases cured, a variety of ailments, other drugs and chemical additives proved to be highly dangerous, and even deadly! Cyclamates, a commonly used artificial sweetener, were found to cause cancer and birth defects. Triparanol, marketed as a blood-cholesterol controller, was discovered to cause baldness and blindness. Chloramphenicol, used to combat minor bacterial infections and more severe illnesses, was found to cause aplastic anemia, a life-threatening ailment. Since the 1950s, thalidomide had been marketed in countries across the globe as a cure for morning sickness in pregnant women. Before it was approved for use in the United States by the Food and Drug Administration (FDA), it was discovered that thalidomide also caused birth defects. Unfortunately, thousands of sample thalidomide tablets already had been dispensed nationally by doctors to patients, with tragic results for many children who were born with underdeveloped limbs and other physical anomalies as a result of exposure to the drug.

Other medical and health-related challenges were faced during the decade. They included combating a rubella (German measles) epidemic that swept across the country; making affordable medical care available to the nation's poor and elderly; acknowledging and publicizing the health risks, including contracting cancer and heart disease, which were associated with use of tobacco products; and recognizing the threat of environmental pollution to the future of civilization. Before the decade ended, a rubella vaccine was perfected. An attempt to offer health care to all Americans came with the introduction of the federal Medicare and Medicaid programs. Efforts were made to begin educating the public about the health risks linked to tobacco and the importance of eliminating industrial pollutants from the environment.

Denton A. Cooley (1920–) During the 1960s, Denton A. Cooley became one of the world's primary practitioners of open-heart surgery. Previously, he had worked with Michael DeBakey on the development of procedures to remove aortic aneurysms (sacs formed on the walls of arteries), and had completed pioneering work in the area of repairing congenital heart defects. In 1968, Cooley performed the world's second person-to-person heart-transplant operation. The following year, he earned his greatest fame by performing the first complete artificial heart transplant. By 1972, Cooley had performed more than ten thousand open-heart operations. *Photo reproduced by permission of the Corbis Corporation.*

Irving S. Cooper (1922–1985) During the early 1960s, Irving S. Cooper began employing a technique he helped perfect, cryosurgery (surgery by freezing), to treat patients afflicted with Parkinson's disease, a neurological disorder. Cryosurgery is carried out by using a probe that has been chilled by liquid nitrogen to nearly 400 degrees below zero Fahrenheit. The probe kills the diseased tissue by freezing it, resulting in an improvement in the patient's muscular control. In 1973, Cooper perfected another medical innovation: a brain implant whose electric impulses assisted patients suffering from epileptic seizures, spasms caused by cerebral palsy, and poststroke paralysis.

Michael E. DeBakey (1908–) Michael E. DeBakey was one of the era's pioneering cardiovascular researchers and surgeons. He was a primary leader in the development of the artificial heart. As early as 1965, he forecast the implementation of permanent artificial hearts. Among DeBakey's earlier accomplishments were the development of a pump that was a precursor of the heart-lung machines later employed during open-heart surgery, and the implementation of Mobile Army Surgical Hospital (M.A.S.H.) units that performed medical procedures close to battlefronts during World War II (1939–45). In 1936, he pointed out the link between smoking and lung cancer. *Photo reproduced courtesy of the Library of Congress.*

Harry F. Harlow (1905–1981) By studying the social activities of monkeys, psychologist Harry F. Harlow provided new understanding of human behavior and development. His experiments with newborn rhesus monkeys (which are more mature at birth than human beings) determined they required nursing, contact, and cuddling from their mothers. Additionally, they needed to play and socialize with other monkeys. Harlow's findings altered then-current thinking about animal development and learning and influenced the understanding of the developmental phases of infancy and childhood in human beings, as well. *Photo reproduced by permission of the University of Wisconsin Harlow Primate Laboratory.*

Frances Oldham Kelsey (1914–) In 1960, the Richardson-Merrill pharmaceutical company submitted an application to the Food and Drug Administration (FDA) to market thalidomide under the brand name Kevadon. Frances Oldham Kelsey, a newly hired FDA medical reviewer, was asked to evaluate the application. Richardson-Merrill pressured Kelsey for quick approval since thalidomide already was being used in other countries. Kelsey repeatedly requested additional data on the drug, forestalling approval. When thalidomide was acknowledged to cause birth defects, Kelsey emerged as a heroine. Her careful analysis and refusal to cave in to drug industry pressure forever changed the way drugs are evaluated and sanctioned for use in the United States. *Photo reproduced courtesy of the Library of Congress.*

Luther L. Terry (1911–1985) Luther L. Terry is best remembered as the U.S. Surgeon General who presided over the committee whose findings linked cigarette smoking to poor health. These conclusions directly affected Terry. Before the study began, the surgeon general was himself a cigarette smoker. By its conclusion, he had switched to a pipe (which was considered far less hazardous). After his term concluded in 1965, Terry was at the forefront of a campaign to ban cigarette advertising on television and radio, which succeeded in the early 1970s. He also crusaded for the control of smoking in the workplace. *Photo reproduced by permission of AP/Wide World Photos.*

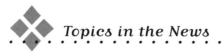

Topics in the News

❖ MORE CARS EQUAL MORE SMOG

One of the downsides to the automobile boom of the 1950s and 1960s was deteriorating air quality, particularly in the nation's most heavily traveled communities. In the 1950s, the California Institute of Technology estimated that 70 percent of the brown haze, called smog, that permeated the air in the Los Angeles area was the byproduct of automobile usage. In 1960, the California state legislature enacted a law requiring all cars to be equipped with an apparatus that would limit noxious fuel emissions.

Air pollution eventually became a national issue. In 1965, Congress passed the Motor Vehicle Air Pollution Control Act, which established national emission standards for cars. The Air Quality Act of 1967 allowed the federal government complete responsibility for air quality.

❖ ARTIFICIAL HEARTS AND HEART TRANSPLANTS

The great advances in the field of cardiovascular (heart) surgery ranked high among the health care-related marvels of the 1960s. During the decade, efforts were made to develop an artificial heart to be employed during surgery when a patient's heart was not completely functional. Early experiments focused on a plastic, banana-shaped apparatus whose valves assisted the blood in its movement between the machine and the patient. However, the machine's pump was found to cause blood clots. Then a similar-looking device was developed that would be implanted permanently in the chest cavity of patients suffering from acute heart failure. This machine was developed by Adrian Kantrowitz (1918–) of Maimonides Hospital in Brooklyn, New York. It first was implanted in February 1965, but the patient died within twenty-four hours. A second procedure was slightly more successful. The pump operated properly; however, the patient died of a stroke twelve days after the implant. In 1966, Michael DeBakey (1908–) successfully implanted a pump in the heart of a patient suffering from rheumatic fever (a communicable disease that causes an inflammation of the heart valves). This pump was different from the one developed by Kantrowitz in that it provided temporary aid to hearts with diseased valves and other irregularities. It supported the left ventricle, the area of the heart that pumps reoxygenated blood to the body.

In 1969, Denton Cooley (1920–) became the first surgeon to place a complete artificial heart in a patient. Cooley and his associates had been attempting to perfect an artificial heart for a decade; for the operation, he

Heart transplants and artificial hearts may have earned the bulk of the headlines, but they were not the only ground-breaking operating room procedures developed during the decade. As the 1960s began, major transplant surgery only involved the kidneys. By decade's end, the first liver and lung transplants had been performed.

While the recipients died, the operations were important first steps in the development of these procedures. Moreover, during the decade, limbs that had been severed during accidents were reattached successfully.

used a device designed by a colleague, Domingo Liotta (1924–). It was the approximate size of a real heart and was composed of Silastic, a silicone plastic. First Cooley attempted to remove the damaged part of the heart and mend it using a Dacron graft (transplant). However, the heart completely stopped beating. Cooley removed it in its entirety, temporarily placed the patient on a heart-lung machine, and then installed the artificial heart. The patient regained consciousness and even was able to speak, but died thirty hours later of pneumonia and kidney failure. At the time, Cooley and DeBakey both were affiliated with the Baylor University College of Medicine. DeBakey was angered by Cooley's decision to perform the operation without consulting him and even accused Cooley of stealing his research. This dispute resulted in Cooley's decision to resign from Baylor and move to the University of Texas at Houston.

In 1967, Christiaan Barnard (1922–2001) of South Africa performed the first successful heart transplant operation, relocating a heart from one human being to another. The following year, Cooley became the first American to complete the procedure. He transplanted the heart of a just-deceased fifteen-year-old girl, whose brain had been damaged during a suicide attempt, into the body of a forty-seven-year-old man. The patient initially recovered, but died 204 days later.

Among the decade's other breakthroughs in the field of cardiovascular surgery: the development of the coronary artery bypass, using a method called revascularization (which guided the flow of blood from the heart's nonessential left internal mammary artery, avoiding diseased arteries); a more sophisticated bypass technique, employed when more than one of

New Methods of Combating Disease

Outside the operating room, a host of new machinery greatly simplified the treatment of disease. One involved the process known as dialysis, in which the blood of patients suffering from kidney failure is removed, cleansed of its poisons, and returned to the body. Without dialysis, the patient will die of uremia (named for a toxic substance that builds up in the blood). Dialysis required the use of expensive equipment, and twice-a-week visits to the hospital. During the decade, the introduction of home dialysis machines significantly reduced the cost of, and time required for, the procedure.

the heart's three main arteries needed repair; and endarterectomy, a technique employed to remove cholesterol and fatty materials that had built up over time in the inside walls of arteries. Researchers also developed the hand-pump (or closed-chest) massage, a technique used to revive victims of heart failure. The hands are employed to rhythmically apply and release pressure over the lower section of the victim's breastbone. The pressure pushes the chest cavity down, squeezing blood out of the heart and allowing it to flow. This method is commonly known as cardiopulmonary resuscitation (CPR).

❖ THE DEMISE OF THE HOUSE CALL

For decades in the United States, a worried parent would contact the family doctor to set an appointment for the examination of a sick child. At the set hour, the parent did not have to bundle up the youngster for the trip to the doctor's office. Instead, the doctor traveled to the family's home to look at the afflicted child.

Prior to World War II (1939–45), approximately 40 percent of doctor-patient contact consisted of physicians making what were known as "house calls." By the beginning of the 1960s, that number had declined to 10 percent. At the decade's close, house calls had become practically extinct. Many in the general population, particularly the elderly and parents of young children, lamented the demise of the house call. They might have been soothed by the presence of the doctor at their bedside, bothered

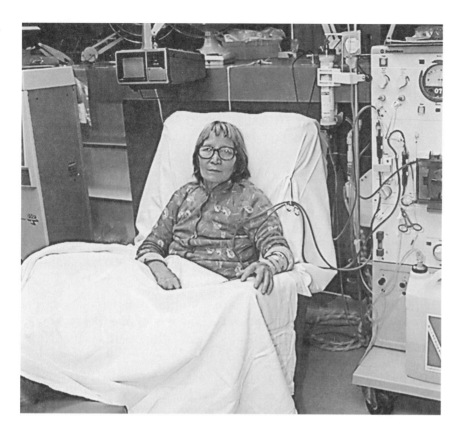

*The demise of the house
call benefited patients
who needed use of large
machinery, such as the
dialysis machine, which
could not be transported
to a patient's home.*
**Reproduced by permission
of PhotoEdit.**

by the inconvenience of trekking to the doctor's office, or convinced that physicians who came to their homes somehow were more caring. However, doctors had come to view house calls as medically ineffective. The time spent traveling from house to house might be better spent treating patients. During house calls, doctors were hampered by the limited equipment they could carry in their medical bag. All the new machinery and drugs that had been developed, and that allowed doctors to more accurately diagnose illnesses, could not be transported from patient to patient.

To convince the population that the demise of the house call was beneficial to patients, the American Medical Association (AMA) issued a public service message in 1964. The point of the message was to illustrate how the house call had become as outdated as the horse-drawn carriage. The message read in part,

> In granddad's time, ol' Doc Brown dashed into the dark of night in his horse and buggy to reach a sick patient on the old homestead. Those days are gone forever, and you can be glad of it! Doc Brown was a good doctor for his time, but often there was little he could do—either in the home or in his office—with the few pills and tonics in his little black

bag. There were no diagnostic laboratories, no x rays, no vast array of wonder drugs, none of the innumerable testing and treatment devices that modern medicine now makes available to your family doctor. Today he can give you much better care in his well-equipped office....

❖ THE OBLIGATION TO SAVE THE PLANET

One of the offshoots of the 1960s anti-Vietnam war protest movement was an increased awareness of the manner in which industrial wastes were polluting the environment. Just a few years earlier, in the 1950s, it might have been fun for a child growing up in a mill town to guess the color of water in the stream flowing through town. Each day, the color would change, depending upon the excess dye that the local textile factory was dumping into the water. No one gave a thought to the effect those chemicals were having on the environment in general and, even more specifically, how it might be affecting the very water that child drank.

During the 1960s, environmental pollution awareness was directly linked to student activism. Interest in the environment grew quickly throughout the decade. The inaugural Earth Day, held on August 22, 1970, involved 1,500 colleges and 10,000 schools. Nevertheless, young people were not the only participants; *Time* magazine reported that 20,000,000 individuals of all ages participated in the event. In describing the first Earth Day, *Audubon* magazine noted, "Now, suddenly, everybody is a conservationist."

When manufacturers were first reproached for polluting the environment, their general response was defensive. They claimed that the protestors were communist-inspired, anticapitalist, and antibig business. However, environmental pollution was a problem that transcended profit-and-loss statements and political agendas. The work of environmentalists during the 1960s was rewarded on January 1, 1970, when President Richard Nixon (1913–1994) signed into law the National Environmental Policy Act of 1969. One of its provisions was the creation of the Environmental Protection Agency (EPA), which coordinates government activity relating to environmental issues and serves as the public's defender in pollution-related disputes.

❖ MAKING HEALTH CARE AVAILABLE TO ALL

One consequence of advances in medical technology was a steep increase in the cost of medical care. New surgical procedures and diagnostic machinery were expensive. While the medical profession is a for-profit business, illness does not play favorites with regard to the size of a patient's wallet. How might the poor, the working class, and the elderly be able to afford top-quality medical care?

As part of his Great Society initiative, President Lyndon Johnson (1908–1973) called for the establishment of the Medicare and Medicaid health care programs. Medicare went into effect in 1966. At its inception, it assisted America's elderly with the cost of hospitalization, home nursing service, outpatient diagnostic testing, and nursing home care. In addition, senior citizens could voluntarily pay a nominal monthly fee of $3 to partially cover perscription drug costs and doctors' visits. Medicaid, meanwhile, was designed to address the health care needs of the poor.

Consumer groups, unions, and senior citizens' organizations lauded Medicaid and Medicare. However, organized medicine like the American Medical Association (AMA), insurance companies, and the majority of doctors vehemently opposed them. They categorized Medicare and Medicaid as "socialized medicine" and contrary to the tenets of free enterprise. Before the decade ended, Medicaid succeeded in significantly raising health care costs because health services were being extended to individuals who previously had not sought medical care. The system was beleaguered by cost overruns and well-publicized bureaucratic bungling. Scandals resulted when health care professionals cheated the system by overbilling for services rendered. In an effort to halt the swift rise in physician fees, the U.S. government froze fee schedules paid under the program. This led to many doctors simply refusing to accept Medicaid patients.

❖ MEASLES: NO ORDINARY ILLNESS

Back in the 1960s, measles, along with such maladies as chicken pox, mumps, and tonsillitis, was viewed as a routine childhood affliction. Measles was a communicable disease, caused by a virus, which resulted in fever, skin rash, and inflammation of the mucus membrane in the nose. Most youngsters contracted the disease; an adult's infection was considered far more critical. Nevertheless, measles was a serious disease for children. Each year, approximately four hundred Americans, mostly youngsters, died of measles. One out of every four thousand children who contracted the disease recovered physically but ended up mentally challenged. During the late 1950s, John Enders (1897–1985), a virologist (specialist in viruses) connected with Harvard University, isolated the measles virus. In 1961, he and his colleagues perfected a live-virus measles vaccine that offered nearly 100 percent immunity and saved tens of thousands of lives throughout the world.

The destructive nature of measles was never more apparent than between 1963 and 1965, when an epidemic of rubella (German measles)

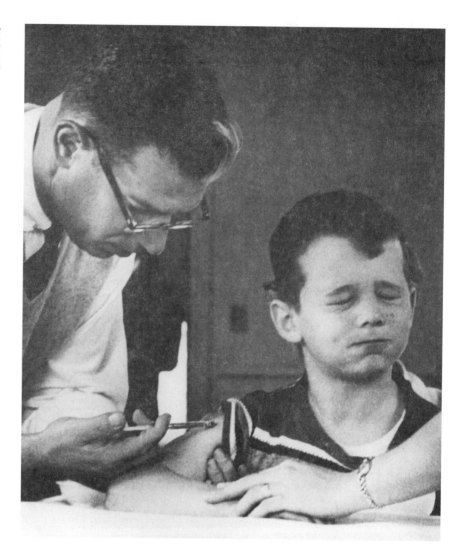

*The measles vaccine
ended the measles and
rubella epidemics during
the mid-1960s. Reproduced
by permission of AP/Wide
World Photos.*

swept across America. German measles also was contagious, and the
afflicted individual suffered from sore throat, pain in the limbs, small skin
rashes, and slight fever. While considered less severe than measles, rubella
still caused long-lasting suffering among the thousands who were afflicted. A reported 30,000 pregnant women who contracted the disease suffered miscarriages (the premature delivery of the fetus, which does not
live). An additional 20,000 gave birth to babies who suffered severe abnor-
malities, including blindness, deafness, limb and heart defects, and mental
illness. Three different groups of researchers succeeded in isolating the
rubella virus, which was the first step toward developing a vaccine. A test
was also devised that would determine one's immunity to the disease. The

actual development of a vaccine proved more complicated. One vaccine, made with a killed virus, proved unsuccessful. Another, which included a live virus, succeeded only in giving people rubella. A third consisted of an attenuated (weakened) virus, which was grown in the kidney cells of monkeys. This version was tested on sixteen youngsters at the Arkansas Children's Colony for mentally challenged children. It was given with their parents' permission. Half were administered the vaccine, and half served as controls. The test proved successful. The Food and Drug Administration (FDA) approved this vaccine in 1969.

❖ SEX: MEDICAL (AND MORAL) ISSUES

With regard to religion and morality, feminism, and contemporary lifestyles, the sexual revolution that swept across the country during the 1960s was liberating to many women's rights advocates and upsetting to religious conservatives. However, it brought to light a host of health-related issues.

At the forefront of the sexual revolution was the availability of newly marketed birth control devices, which allowed women to take charge of their bodies, and their sexual behavior. One was the intrauterine device (IUD), which was made of plastic, nylon, or stainless steel. A doctor placed an IUD within the uterus of the patient, where it could be left for years. By 1963, more than 20,000 American women relied on IUDs. However, on occasion, they were known to cause heavy bleeding, and even severe, life-threatening infections.

Birth control pills also became wildly popular during the decade and, similarly, aside from the moral debate surrounding their use, their long-term side effects were unknown. Critics claimed that users of "The Pill" risked contracting breast and uterine cancer, allegations that were unsubstantiated. Before the decade ended, however, one potential threat was verified. Women over thirty-five who smoked and used birth control pills had a higher risk of suffering heart attacks, strokes, and blood clots in vessels that travel to the lungs.

The general increase in sexual activity that occurred during the decade also resulted in a rise in unwanted pregnancy. Throughout the decade, abortion was illegal in the United States. (In forty-five states, the procedure was allowed only if the pregnant woman's life was judged to be in danger; during the decade, Colorado passed a law allowing abortion in the case of incest or rape.) If a woman were desperate to abort a fetus, she often had no alternative but to have the procedure carried out illegally. A woman of means and with connections might be able to find a surgeon to perform the operation for a hefty fee. However, most abortions were performed by amateurs employing dangerous methods in less-than-sterile conditions.

On the other hand, many women wished to become pregnant but were unable to do so. During earlier eras, their only choice for parenthood involved adoption. However, during the 1960s, two effective drugs were developed in Europe—one in Sweden and the other in Italy—that combated infertility in women by stimulating the ovaries to prepare and release eggs. The Italian drug, called pergonal, was tested by researchers at New York's Columbia-Presbyterian Medical Center. Fifteen of twenty-one infertile women who were administered the drug became pregnant. Of the first seven who delivered, three had twins and one had quadruplets!

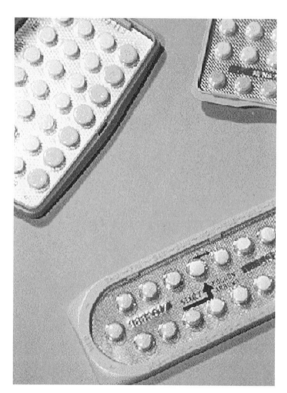

Additionally, a technique called artificial insemination became more widely available during the 1960s, although it was considered controversial by some. There were legislators and religious leaders who wanted to outlaw the procedure, calling it a form of adultery. In cases where a husband was infertile (unable to produce children), the wife would receive a donor's sperm that had been frozen and stored for such a use. In 1960, between 1,000 and 1,200 babies were artificially conceived. These numbers increased as the years passed and legal challenges to the procedure declined.

Finally, the process by which women gave birth began to change significantly. Before World War II (1939–45), the majority of women gave birth at home. After the war, hospital births became more common. New drugs made the process less painful, and allowed doctors more control over the procedure.

The birth control pill allowed women greater sexual and reproductive freedom. Reproduced by permission of Archive Photos, Inc.

Although childbirth became safer in some ways, these changes caused women to become passive participants in one of the most significant events of their lives. While in labor, women were administered pain-reducing anesthesia agents. Near the conclusion, they were rendered unconscious by general anesthesia. Since they were unable to push the baby out, a physician employed forceps (large steel tongs) to complete the birth. However, studies in the 1950s and 1960s revealed that babies appeared to be affected negatively by the drugs their mothers took during pregnancy, and by the anesthetics administered during delivery. The use of forceps also occasionally caused injury to the baby.

As women began to expect to have greater control over their bodies by the end of the 1960s, interest grew in the natural childbirth techniques that had been pioneered in the 1950s by Fernand Lamaze (1890–1957), a French obstetrician. Pregnant women learned special breathing techniques to control pain during birth. They were prepared psychologically to undergo the process, and were given matter-of-fact information regarding pregnancy and childbirth. Among the tenets of Lamaze birth: "Women's inner wisdom guides them through birth"; "Birth is normal, natural, and healthy"; and "Childbirth education empowers women to make informed choices in healthcare.… "

Lamaze education and "natural childbirth" preparation were not widely accepted or available in the United States until the next decade. However, many young women in the later years of the 1960s pursued the opportunity to become educated about the details of childbirth, actively assist in childbirth, and ultimately, contribute to the well-being of their children through these methods and techniques.

❖ SUGAR SUBSTITUTES: THE BITTER WITH THE SWEET

In the mid-1960s, individuals who wished to cut down on their sugar intake could choose from two chemical substitutes: saccharin and cyclamates. Both were extremely sweet. Saccharin often left a bitter aftertaste, while cyclamates did not. But during the latter years of the decade, it became known that continuous use of cyclamates could be deadly!

Cyclamates were introduced on the market during the 1950s. By the following decade, they were added to soft drinks, canned fruit, salad dressings, and candy. Between 1963 and 1970, national consumption of cyclamates rose from 5 million to 21 million pounds annually. In 1966, Food and Drug Administration (FDA) research determined that cyclamates caused birth defects in 15 percent of the chicks born to chickens exposed to the drug. It also caused chromosome breaks in rats that were fed high doses and cancer in other animals. Still, both the FDA and Abbott Labs, which produced cyclamates, decreed that the product was safe. A fiery public debate ensued. Eventually, all products containing cyclamates were ordered off supermarket shelves by February 1, 1970.

❖ THALIDOMIDE: A GLOBAL TRAGEDY

Thalidomide first was developed in the United States as a possible anti-seizure drug. Eventually, Chemie Gruenenthal, a West German drug company, took over testing and found it to be effective as a sedative. Additionally, it relieved nausea (or morning sickness) in many women during the early stages of pregnancy. By 1957, Chemie Gruenenthal was marketing

Drugs and Their Side Effects

Just as the tragic side effects of thalidomide were determined, it was discovered that other drugs also caused unwanted, unexpected problems. For example, triparanol, marketed in 1959 as a blood cholesterol controller, was found to cause baldness and blindness. Richardson-Merrill, the company that marketed the drug, discovered the blindness side effect while testing the drug on laboratory rats and dogs. However, the company failed to note these findings to the FDA when requesting approval to market the drug. The FDA eventually brought charges against Richardson-Merrill and three former executives.

Another drug, chloramphenicol, was useful in battling meningitis and certain rare, tropical diseases. It also was prescribed for minor bacterial infections. As early as 1952, chloramphenicol was found to cause anemia (low counts of red blood cells); eventually, the side effect was upgraded to aplastic anemia, a life-threatening ailment in which blood cells cease being produced within the body. Parke, Davis and Company had marketed the drug under the name Chloromycetin. Still, in 1968, between $70 million and $80 million worth of the drug still was being prescribed, mostly to combat colds and acne.

thalidomide over the counter in West Germany. Three years later, it was available throughout Europe, as well as in Canada and South America.

However, as thalidomide use increased, physicians began noting the appearance of a rare type of birth defect among the offspring of its users: phocomelia (literally "seal limbs"), in which the limbs of the fetus improperly form. For example, the baby might be born without an arm, or with a hand protruding from its shoulder. Babies also were entering the world with kidney problems, heart defects, and deafness. All these problems eventually were traced to the use of thalidomide. In fact, more than ten thousand children in forty-six countries were estimated to have been born with thalidomide-related deformities. In 1961, the drug was banned in West Germany.

The previous year, Richardson-Merrill, a pharmaceutical company, submitted an application to the Food and Drug Administration (FDA) to market thalidomide in the United States. At the time, FDA regulations allowed doctors to distribute free samples of drugs being considered for approval. Before its side effects were noted, Richardson-Merrill distributed an undetermined number of thalidomide tablets, some estimates were that it was as high as 2,500,000, to more than 1,000 doctors to dispense as samples. Reportedly, nearly 20,000 patients, including pregnant women, received them. FDA employees contacted the doctors and urged them to inform those who had received the samples. Unfortunately, not all doctors maintained records pertaining to the drug's distribution. An undetermined number of deformed infants were born in the United States to mothers who had taken thalidomide.

As knowledge of the effects of the drug became known, the tragedy brought forth questions about the fairness of antiabortion laws that forced some women to give birth to children they knew would be seriously handicapped.

❖ SMOKING AND HEALTH

By the early 1960s, scientists had become convinced that the use of tobacco products could be linked directly to the spread of cancer. However, two groups were dead-set against admitting this connection. The nation's tobacco growers wished to continue to thrive monetarily; at the time, tobacco was an $8 million a year industry. Plus, the economic survival of the nation's southern states depended upon a steady tobacco crop and a market of buyers. Together, both groups constituted a powerful political lobby. Politicians from these states, influenced in no small part by the tobacco industry, united to crush the dissemination of information relating cigarettes to ill health.

In 1962, President John F. Kennedy (1917–1963) asked U.S. Surgeon General Luther Terry (1911–1985) to examine the relationship between the use of tobacco products and the nation's health. Instead of commissioning a survey, Terry appointed a ten-person Advisory Committee on Smoking and Health to examine preexisting research. On the committee were three cigarette smokers, along with one pipe smoker and one cigar smoker. The committee spent two years poring over thousands of articles and reports on file at the National Medical Library in Bethesda, Maryland. Its members examined animal laboratory studies, human autopsy reports, clinical evaluations of patients, and statistical analyses. Their findings—issued in January 1964, in a 150,000-word, 387-page report—were presented on a Saturday morning, in order to prevent the result from immediately impacting on tobacco industry stock market prices.

Terry's committee found that cigarette smoking in general increased the death rate and caused a range of potentially fatal illnesses, starting with lung cancer, heart disease, and emphysema. The more one smoked, the more susceptible one was to these maladies. When one gave up smoking, the health risks decreased. While cigar and pipe smoking seemed less perilous than cigarette smoking, their usage seemed to slightly raise the risk of developing lip cancer. The sole positive note in the report was that smokers benefited psychologically from the pleasure they received from puffing cigarettes. The committee advised that "appropriate remedial action is warranted" in relation to the clear link between cigarette use and maintaining one's health. In response, tobacco growers and politicians from tobacco-growing states banded together to defame the report. Their power and influence were far-reaching. For example, at the time, tobacco products were marketed in commercials that regularly aired on television. After the release of the report, the National Interagency Council on Smoking and Health recommended a complete ban on cigarette advertising. Oddly, the American Medical Association (AMA) opposed the ban. Then it was revealed that the AMA had accepted a large monetary grant from the tobacco industry to conduct a five-year study of smoking and health.

In wake of the publicity surrounding the report, cigarette sales decreased by approximately 10 percent and cigarette company stock prices fell. However, both declines were temporary. Total cigarette sales in 1964 were just 3 percent less than the previous year, and stock prices climbed to previous levels. Meanwhile, in 1963, the American Heart Association announced the commencement of an antismoking campaign. The following year, the Federal Trade Commission ordered that, beginning in 1965, health warnings must be featured on cigarette packaging. Legislators from tobacco-growing states vehemently opposed the various bills that were being debated in Congress regarding the nature of these warnings. Eventually, a compromise was reached. Beginning in January 1966, cigarette manufacturers were required to include the following advisory on all cigarette packaging: "Caution: Cigarette smoking may be hazardous to your health."

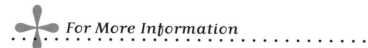 *For More Information*

BOOKS

Andryszewski, Tricia. *Abortion: Rights, Options, and Choices.* Brookfield, CT: Millbrook Press, 1996.

Archer, Jules. *To Save the Earth: The American Environmental Movement.* New York: Viking Press, 1998.

Berger, Melvin. *The Artificial Heart.* New York: Franklin Watts, 1987.

Clayton, Lawrence, Ph.D. *Tranquilizers.* Springfield, NJ: Enslow Publishers, 1997.

Currie, Stephen. *Abortion.* San Diego, CA: Greenhaven Press, 2000.

Day, Nancy. *Killer Superbugs: The Story of Drug-Resistant Diseases.* Berkeley Heights, NJ: Enslow Publishers, 2001.

De Angelis, Gina. *Nicotine and Cigarettes.* Philadelphia: Chelsea House, 1999.

Durrett, Deanne. *The Abortion Conflict: A Pro/Con Issue.* Berkeley Heights, NJ: Enslow Publishers, 2000.

Gay, Kathlyn. *Pregnancy: Private Decisions, Public Debates.* New York: Franklin Watts, 1994.

Gold, Susan Dudley. *Roe V. Wade: Abortion.* New York: Twenty-First Century Books, 1994.

Herda, D. J. *Roe V. Wade: The Abortion Question.* Hillside, NJ: Enslow Publishers, 1994.

Lassieur, Allison. *Abortion.* San Diego, CA: Lucent Books, 2001.

Lowenstein, Felicia. *The Abortion Battle: Looking at Both Sides.* Springfield, NJ: Enslow Publishers, 1996.

Netzley, Patricia D. *Issues in the Environment.* San Diego, CA: Lucent Books, 1998.

Morgan, Sally. *Smoking.* Austin, TX: Raintree Steck-Vaughn, 2002.

Pringle, Laurence. *The Environmental Movement: From Its Roots to the Challenges of a New Century.* New York: HarperCollins Juvenile Books, 2000.

Pringle, Laurence. *Smoking: A Risky Business.* New York: Morrow Junior Books, 1996.

Robbins, Ocean, and Sol Solomon. *Choices for Our Future: A Generation Rising for Life.* Summertown, TN: Book Pub Co., 1994.

Roleff, Tamara L., ed. *Abortion: Opposing Viewpoints.* San Diego, CA: Greenhaven Press, 1997.

Roleff, Tamara L., and Mary E. Williams, eds. *Tobacco and Smoking: Opposing Viewpoints.* San Diego, CA: Greenhaven Press, 1998.

Romaine, Deborah H. *Roe V. Wade: Abortion and the Supreme Court.* San Diego, CA: Lucent Books, 1998.

Silverstein, Alvin, Virginia Silverstein, and Robert Silverstein. *Measles and Rubella.* Springfield, NJ: Enslow Publishers, 1997.

Stefoff, Rebecca. *The American Environmental Movement.* New York: Facts on File, 1995.

Terry, Luther L., and Daniel Horn. *To Smoke or Not to Smoke.* New York: Lothrop Lee & Shepard, 1969.

Williams, Mary E., ed. *Abortion: Opposing Viewpoints.* San Diego, CA: Greenhaven Press, 2001.

WEB SITES

The Man Who Saved Your Life—Maurice R. Hilleman. http://www.njabr.org/superstars/hilleman/hilleman8.cfm (accessed on August 6, 2002).

The Women's Health Movement from the 1960s to the Present, and Beyond. http://www.4woman.gov/owh/pub/history/healthmvmt.htm (accessed on August 6, 2002).

chapter seven **Science and Technology**

1960 A synthetic ruby is used to produce a laser.

1960: Artificial suntanning cream is developed.

1960: The solar system is estimated to be 4.9 billion years old.

1960: The USS *George Washington,* a state-of-the-art nuclear-powered submarine, is launched.

1960: April 1 *Tiros 1,* the first weather satellite, is launched.

1961: The USS *Enterprise* aircraft carrier, run by eight nuclear reactors, is launched.

1961: Texas Instruments patents the first silicon chip used for electronic circuits.

1961: January 3 Three maintenance crew members are killed by a nuclear explosion in the Stationary Low Power Reactor Number One at the U.S. Atomic Energy Commission's National Reactor Testing Station in Idaho Falls, Idaho.

1961: January 31 The National Aeronautics and Space Administration (NASA) launches into space a capsule containing a chimpanzee, and successfully recovers the animal.

1961: April Chemists form Element 103 (lawrencium), a radioactive chemical element, by showering californium with boron nuclei.

1961: April 12 Cosmonaut Yuri A. Gagarin becomes the first Russian launched into space.

1961: May 5 Astronaut Alan B. Shepard Jr. becomes the first American launched into space.

1962: The U.S. scientific space probe *Mariner 2* reaches Venus 109 days after its launch.

1962: Kelvinator produces a dishwasher that employs high-frequency sound waves, rather than soap and water.

1962: Powdered orange juice is patented.

1962: June 16 Cosmonaut Valentina V. Tereshkova becomes the first woman in space.

1963: The USS *Atlantis II* clearly photographs the ocean floor.

1964: The Verrazano Narrows Bridge, the world's largest suspension bridge, opens in New York City.

1964: IBM produces a new product, the word processor, a hybrid of the typewriter and computer.

1964: August 5 Congress establishes the National Commission on Technology,

Automation and Economic Progress, to analyze the impact of automation on unemployment.

1965: Traffic control in Chicago, New York, and Detroit becomes computerized.

1965: A computer at the New York Stock Exchange answers questions over the telephone using an artificial voice.

1965: February 17 *Ranger 8,* a moon probe, blasts off into space and sends back more than seven thousand images of the moon's surface before crashing into the lunar Sea of Tranquility.

1965: July 15 *Mariner 4* sends the first close-up photographs of Mars.

1966: Radar is used to measure the polar ice thickness.

1966: June 2 *Sorcerer I* makes the first soft landing on the moon.

1967: Computer keyboards are developed, allowing immediate access between the operator and the computer.

1967: RCA develops a compact television camera weighing just over two pounds.

1967: A cordless, battery-powered telephone is developed.

1967: A solar-powered house is built.

1967: January 27 A launch pad fire kills American astronauts Virgil "Gus" Grissom, Edward H. White, and Roger B. Chaffee during a test for what would have been the first space mission with a three-person crew on board.

1967: March 1 The first overseas direct telephone dialing begins.

1968: Scientists use radar to map the surface of Venus.

1968: The picosecond, the smallest period of time detectable, is measured at Bell Laboratories.

1968: August 16 The *Poseidon 3,* a new missile that can be launched from submarines, is tested.

1968: October 11 *Apollo 7,* the first manned Apollo flight, begins a seven-day mission.

1969: January 22 The Atomic Energy Commission announces completion of the world's largest superconducting magnet.

1969: July 16 *Apollo 11* is launched. This flight culminates in the landing of the first human on the surface of the moon.

1969: November 18 Americans land on the moon for the second time in *Apollo 12.*

Overview

Before the 1960s, space travel was considered to be pure fantasy, the subject of science fiction novels and films conjured up by writers with vivid imaginations. However, the beginning of the decade saw the first human beings flying through space and orbiting the Earth. In April 1961, Russian cosmonaut Yuri A. Gagarin became the first man in space, orbiting the Earth in a 108-minute flight on board the *Vostok I* spacecraft. Less than a month later, astronaut Alan B. Shepard became the first American in space. His flight lasted 14 minutes and 28 seconds. Before the decade ended, human beings had landed on the moon. Neil A. Armstrong, one of three astronauts participating in the *Apollo 11* mission, became the first to set foot on the moon's surface. It was the 1960's most highly publicized scientific and technological achievement. In one of the decade's most celebrated quotes, Armstrong noted, as he set foot on the moon, "That's one small step for man, one giant leap for mankind." The date was July 20, 1969.

Exploration of the heavens was not limited to humans traveling in spaceships and landing on the moon. Satellites were launched into outer space throughout the decade. As they circled Earth, they performed a range of functions, from relaying live television signals across the oceans to recording weather patterns. During the 1960s, astronomers increased knowledge of the solar system by measuring distances between planets and mapping out their surfaces. They observed cosmic events, newly discovered stars, and quasars (the most distant objects from Earth).

While astronomers were investigating the nature of the heavens and astronauts, cosmonauts, and satellites were orbiting Earth, scientists were also exploring the depths of the ocean floor. Forms of life were discovered in deep seas where none were thought possible. It was determined that, over the course of time, the ocean floor was widening. Three *Sealab* expeditions to the ocean's depths set out to ascertain if individuals could live and work underwater for extended periods of time.

Great strides were made in the evolution of computers. More were produced, and they became more readily available for business and commercial use. While the age of the home computer still was well into the future, the development of silicon chips and integrated computer circuits created an electronics revolution. A range of previously unimaginable devices and products were developed, invented, or patented during the decade, including cordless, battery-powered telephones that were precursors of cell phones, word processing machines, and computer keyboards.

Advances in medicine brought new or improved vaccines for many diseases, including polio, measles, and rubella (German measles). The marketing of the birth control pill also allowed women unprecedented control over their reproductive cycles.

In biology, the first genes (which are the basis of heredity) were isolated, and much was learned about the nature of heredity. Researchers were also striving to learn about the history of our planet. Archeologists and anthropologists devised ways of determining the origin and age of Earth, the manner in which human beings evolved, and the age of artifacts of earlier time periods. The "big bang" theory was thought to explain the origin of the universe. In addition to the focus on Earth's past, scientists devoted attention to the planet's future. Environmental science emerged as a relatively new field of study during the decade. There was increasing concern about the effects of pollution generated through human activity, and the decade saw the first warnings that a greenhouse effect (also known as global warming) could alter Earth's temperature.

Murray Gell-Mann (1929–) In 1961, physicist Murray Gell-Mann developed the theory of the "eightfold way" to explain the "particle zoo" resulting from the discovery of some one hundred new subatomic particles (particles in an atom's nucleus). He showed that all subatomic particles belong to several families, which have similar properties. He also theorized that all subatomic particles are composed of three basic units, which he named *quarks* (a word Gell-Mann took from *Finnegan's Wake* [1930], a novel by James Joyce [1882–1941]). For his work, Gell-Mann received the Nobel Prize in physics in 1969. **Photo reproduced by permission of AP/Wide World Photos.**

John Glenn (1921–) John Glenn became a hero when he piloted America's first orbital flight around Earth in 1962. After being postponed twice due to poor weather conditions, Glenn's Mercury-Atlas rocket, with the space capsule *Friendship* attached, took off from Cape Canaveral on February 20, while millions of Americans watched on national television. After three orbits around Earth, Glenn had to return to the ground due to mechanical difficulties. The flight was considered a success though, and Glenn received a tremendous reception upon his return to Cape Canaveral. President John Kennedy even flew to Florida to congratulate Glenn personally on the flight.

Virgil "Gus" Grissom (1926–1967) Virgil "Gus" Grissom was a key figure in the United States' manned spaceflight program. He became the second American in space in the Project Mercury program. Then he helped design and construct the spacecraft for Project Gemini, and was on board during the first two-man Gemini flight. Grissom made headlines one final time as the focus of a tragedy. He and his copilots Edward H. White (1930–1967) and Roger Chaffee (1935–1967) were engaged in a launch pad test of the first Apollo/Saturn capsule. During the test, a flash fire broke out in the pure oxygen atmosphere on board, killing all three astronauts. **Photo reproduced by permission of the Corbis Corporation.**

Harry H. Hess (1906–1969) When oceanographer Harry H. Hess served in the U.S. Navy, he became intrigued by the presence of flat-topped mountains, located underwater, which were identified by his sonar equipment. He named these mountains "guyots" in honor of Arnold Guyot (1807–1884), the Swiss American who was Princeton University's first professor of geology. Hess determined that the guyots were volcanic islands formed along the mid-ocean ridges. He theorized that they were moving under Earth's continents and pushing the continents apart, gradually widening the ocean's floor.

Marshall W. Nirenberg (1927–) Marshall W. Nirenberg, working at the National Institutes of Health in Bethesda, Maryland, performed groundbreaking experiments in biochemistry during the early 1960s. He successfully produced synthetic protein (polyphenylalanine), which proved to be an important step leading to the discovery of the genetic code (the "instructions" in a gene that tell a cell how to make a specific protein). Nirenberg accomplished this breakthrough by controlling the chemicals he introduced into the test tube and noting the proteins produced. In 1968, Nirenberg shared the Nobel Prize in physiology or medicine for the "interpretation of the genetic code and its function."

Joseph Weber (1919–2000) In 1916, Albert Einstein (1879–1955) shook the physics world with his general theory of relativity. In his theory, Einstein accounted for bodies moving relative to each other at any speed, even if those speeds are changing. Furthermore, Einstein proposed that those bodies give off gravity waves which travel at the speed of light. Einstein's theory generally was accepted by the scientific community. However, it was not until 1968, when physicist Joseph Weber published the results of a ten-year experiment, that these waves were proven to exist. Weber accomplished this by developing a gravitational wave detector, consisting of a large, freely suspended aluminum cylinder, which was able to measure volumes smaller than the size of a nucleus.

◆◆ *Topics in the News* ·

❖ ARCHAEOLOGY/ANTHROPOLOGY: AN AGE OF DISCOVERY

Archeologists and anthropologists have always had difficulty determining the age of rocks, pottery, tools, weapons, and other artifacts of earlier time periods. Two new techniques for accomplishing this emerged during the 1960s. Thermo-luminescence, used to date rocks and pottery as far back as 1,000 years, measures the radioactive elements found in the artifact. This may be achieved when the rock or pot is heated to about 350 degrees Celsius. The other technique employs obsidian: a hard, volcanic rock formed when lava cools. Gray, black, or semitransparent in color, obsidian was scraped and shaped into tools and weapons. Water that touches the surface of obsidian gradually seeps down through the material. As a result, old obsidian has an outer rind that contains water, while its inner parts remain dry. The thickness of this rind can be measured accurately under a microscope. The thicker the rind, the longer it has been since it was made into a tool.

In 1959, British archeologist and anthropologist Louis S. B. Leaky (1903–1972) and his wife Mary (1913–1996) found what Louis claimed was the five-million-year-old "missing link" (an early human ancestor from which evolved one line of apes and another set of descendents which evolved into present-day humans). Their discovery was made in the Olduvai Gorge, an archeological site located in north Tanganyika (now Tanzania). The "link" was a skeleton called the Zinjanthropus, which the Leakeys nicknamed "Zinj."

While this discovery propelled the Leakeys to international fame, many in the archeology and anthropology community doubted Leakeys' claim because "Zinj" seemed so unhuman. Furthermore, during the decade, an even earlier ancestor was found during an expedition sponsored by Yale University's Peabody Museum. Those on the expedition explored the Fayum desert in Egypt, an area that includes ancient lava flows. As wind and rain eroded the lava, various remains were exposed. One of them was the era's most dramatic find: a small, almost-intact skull that belonged to an early ape ancestor named Aegyptopithecus. The skull was found to be between 26 million and 28 million years old.

Then in 1968, the oldest-known amino acids (organic compounds that are the units of structure in proteins) were found in a rock formation located near Barberton, South Africa. The rocks were dated as being 3.1 billon years old, and were the oldest discovered to date. They contained what appeared to be fossils (remains of plants or animals that have been preserved in Earth's crust) of algae and bacteria, some of the earliest forms of life.

❖ ASTRONOMY: FASCINATION WITH THE HEAVENS

In 1964, a radio dish located at Arecibo in Puerto Rico first was used to bounce radio waves off planets in the solar system and detect their return to Earth. This process allowed astronomers to more accurately measure the space between planets and the number of Earth's orbits around the Sun. Meanwhile, three groups of astronomers separately mapped the planet Venus, whose surface cannot be seen by ordinary telescopes because it is covered by clouds. Mountains were discovered on Venus, and the planet's rotation was calculated.

Detectors of infrared rays (which are invisible, and located just beyond the red of the visible spectrum) were used in astronomy during the decade. Infrared astronomy is best accomplished by using high-altitude balloons rather than rockets. The first major infrared astronomical expedition was a manned balloon mission launched by the U.S. Navy in 1959. The infrared telescope was pointed at Venus, but the balloon's design and movement caused by the crewmembers inside it made the mission's results unreliable. In 1961, the U.S. Air Force took over the experiments and switched to unmanned balloons. Two years later, Martin Schwarzchild (1912–1997) of Princeton University launched an unmanned balloon which detected water vapor around Mars. In 1964, an air force-launched balloon uncovered water vapor around Venus.

One of the major astronomy-related discoveries was the quasar (or quasi-stellar object). Quasars are among the most distant objects visible from Earth, and have the energy level of more than one hundred large galaxies. The first identified quasar was 3C-48. (The "3C" stands for Third Cambridge Catalog of Radio Sources, a catalog used by radio astronomers.) Its existence initially was reported in 1960, and astronomers spent the ensuing years identifying its properties. One of those who extensively studied quasars was Margaret Burbridge (1919–) of the University of California, San Diego. She concluded that quasars are galaxies that have passed through each other. Material falls to the center of the quasar where a black hole (a perfect vacuum in space) is located. The black hole sucks everything around it into itself, even light.

Perhaps the most important astronomy-related advancement during the decade was the development of "very long baseline interferometry" (or VLBI), a technique that allowed for the expanded observation of outer space. VLBI was developed in Australia, and came to be used by astronomers around the world. The Australians worked out a mathematical formula that, when applied, allowed astronomers to document signals detected by many radio telescopes, separated from each other by a distance as large as Earth's diameter. These telescopes were linked together to form an enormous antenna. The first practical VLBI system was used at Cambridge University in England in 1960.

Other important events in the world of astronomy included the discovery in outer space of cosmic events called masers (which stands for "microwave amplification by stimulated emission of radiation"), in which narrow but powerful beams of light are emitted; the discovery of pulsars (radio-wave sources with on-off cycles that originate in outer space); and the 1962 launching of the first X-ray detector (a highly sensitive telescope) used in astronomy, from an air force *Aerobee* rocket. Finally, the early 1960s saw the beginning of an ambitious and potentially far-reaching astronomy-related undertaking: Project Ozma, the first modern-day search for other worlds with intelligent life. Project Ozma was named after a princess in the land of Oz, a fantasy world created by children's book author L. Frank Baum (1856–1919). It was carried out by Frank Drake (1930–), working at the National Radio Astronomy Observatory in Green Bank, West Virginia. Employing an 85-foot radio, one of the largest of its time, Drake sent and listened for radio wave messages, hoping to make contact with extraterrestrials. The radio was directed to outer space six hours a day, seven days a week. No life from other worlds was found in Project Ozma.

❖ BIOLOGY: ISOLATING THE GENE, EXPLAINING THE ORIGIN OF LIFE, COMMUNICATING WITH DOLPHINS

During the 1960s, great strides were made in the fields of biochemistry and genetics. By the end of the decade, the first gene was isolated. Genes are the basis of heredity and are carried by DNA (deoxyribonucleic acid). The genetic code had been broken earlier in the decade, so scientists understood how DNA worked. However, the process for isolating genes proved elusive. Jonathan Beckwith (1935–), a biochemist at Harvard University, solved the problem by using two simple viruses, from which he removed the protein shells and heated their DNA. Then he mixed the two together and slowly cooled them. During this process, the DNA from one virus attached itself to the complementary DNA from the other in the only place they fit: the lac gene. Beckwith chemically removed the excess, leaving copies of the complete lac gene intact.

"Primordial soup" was the chemical mixture thought to represent the atmosphere of the early Earth. It was a chemically rich blend, composed of ammonia, hydrogen, methane gas, and water vapor, that was not conducive to living things. Before the 1960s, scientists had begun to illustrate how primordial soup could produce the types of chemicals from which life is made. They continued experimenting with the mixture during the decade. Among their results: a dimer (a combination of two similar chem-

The "big bang" theory is the foremost science-based speculation explaining the origin of the universe. According to the theory, all the elements of the universe came into being between 10 billion and 20 billion years ago as the result of a gigantic cosmic explosion (or "big bang") that flung matter in all directions. The theory was put forward to explain why faraway galaxies are traveling away from Earth at enormous speeds. In addition, after the "bang," leftover energy remained present in outer space.

In 1961, the world's most sensitive radio telescope was employed to send and receive signals from the *Echo* satellite. During this process, astronomers noted a strange electronic noise emanating from the satellite. They eventually concluded that the noise originated in outer space, and was caused by energy that remained from the "big bang." While this was the first solid evidence in support of the "big bang" theory, and the premise is widely accepted, it generally is acknowledged that the theory never can be proved conclusively.

icals) was formed under primitive Earth conditions; ribonucleic acid, or RNA (a chemical found in cells that plays a role in the flow of genetic information), was formed in a test tube; and amino acids (organic compounds that serve as building blocks in proteins and are crucial to human metabolism) were formed in primordial soup.

During the decade, scientists also began studying how dolphins communicate with one another. Dolphins are mammals that breathe with lungs, nurse their young, and have extremely complex brains. Neurophysicist John C. Lilly (1915–2001) implanted electrodes in the brains of thirty dolphins. By stimulating the electrodes, he discovered a "pleasure center" that caused the dolphins to have wide eyes and look as if they are smiling.

In another experiment, Lilly placed a partially paralyzed dolphin in a pool with other dolphins. In order to live, the injured mammal had to swim to the surface to breathe; however, he was incapable of doing so on his own. Lilly observed that the other dolphins learned of his distress by communicating with each other in frequencies above the range of human hearing. Having done so, they helped the injured dolphin reach and stay at the surface. Lilly taped their "talking." When he played it back, at one-quarter speed, he could hear the "mayday" call given by the stricken dolphin. When Lilly played the tape back to the other dolphins, they reacted to the call.

❖ COMPUTER SCIENCE: ONE MACHINE FOR ALL

At the beginning of the 1960s, computers were expensive and difficult to operate. For this reason, most were situated in a central location of a company or institution to provide information or processing services to multiple clients on a rotating basis. Only highly trained programmers could operate them.

Early in the decade, John Kemeny (1926–1992) and Thomas Kurtz (1928–) of Dartmouth College decided to create a student-friendly computer system that would allow all scholars—not just engineering, mathematics, and physics graduate students—access to computers. First, they devised what became known as the Dartmouth Time-Sharing System (DTSS), which permitted a single computer to simultaneously serve many users. Then they wrote the Beginners All-purpose Symbolic Instruction Code (more commonly known as BASIC), a revolutionary, easy-to-understand computer programming language that would become the most commonly used in the world. BASIC had only fourteen command structures to learn. Within two hours, students being trained in BASIC were programming computers. By 1968, 80 percent of Dartmouth students, most of whom were not math or science majors, were programming computers. Kemeny and Kurtz continued to improve BASIC, always keeping it simple to use.

The integrated computer circuit was another innovation that created an electronics revolution. Previously, circuit boards that ran electronic devices had to be large enough to hold such components as resistors, capacitors, and vacuum tubes. The size of circuit boards was first reduced in the 1950s when vacuum tubes were replaced by transistors (small, durable electronic devices used for sound amplification and switching). Then came the development of the semiconductor (an electronics device made from such semiconductor materials as silicon and germanium, whose electrical properties lie between those of conductors and insulators). The small size of the semiconductor allowed for the incorporation of literally hundreds of thousands of individual components onto a single one-inch-square silicon wafer. Computers that once were the size of small bedrooms were reduced to the dimensions of a television set.

Integrated computer circuits first were used by the military. Before the decade ended, they were being employed in the production of such consumer products as television sets and radios.

❖ EARTH SCIENCES: LESS-EXPENSIVE ELECTRICITY AND DIRE PREDICTIONS

Inside Earth is a giant source of heat called geothermal power, which can be employed to operate electrical generators. One of the first geothermal power units was constructed in Larderello, Italy, in the early 1900s. Because of the expense involved in reaching the heat source and carrying it to the surface in usable form, no such plants were built in the United States until the early 1960s. At that time, a pipeline system began shipping 265,000 pounds of steam per hour from the valley of Big Sulphur Creek, located 70 miles north of San Francisco, to an electricity-producing generator constructed by Pacific Gas and Electric. The pipelines carried steam at pressures of one hundred pounds per square inch and temperatures of 348 degrees Fahrenheit. It has been estimated that the geysers located in the valley can continue to supply power at this rate for 11,000 years.

Not all the earth-science-related news during the decade was as positive as the developments in Big Sulphur Creek. In 1964, climatologists Syukuro Manabe and Richard Wetherald of the Geophysical Fluid Dynamics Laboratory in Princeton, New Jersey, developed a computer model of the atmosphere. Their goal was to predict how water vapor and carbon dioxide (which is produced by burning carbon fuel) would affect the climate. Their results, which they published in 1967, came to be known as the greenhouse effect, more commonly known today as global warming. Manabe and Wetherald calculated that a doubling of carbon dioxide in the atmosphere gradually would warm Earth's surface, resulting in massive global climate changes. This increase is directly linked to the burning of man-made fuels.

❖ OCEANOGRAPHY: MOHOLE, TRIESTE, AND SEALAB

While the exploration of outer space earned the bulk of publicity during the 1960s, great strides were made in the area of oceanography, the subdivision of geography that deals with the depths of the ocean.

Earth is composed of three layers: the outer crust, the mantle, and the core. In 1960, oceanographer Harry H. Hess (1906–1969) published his theory that the ocean's floor gradually was widening. Hess's premise was tested when a hole was drilled in the seafloor in order to pierce the Mohorovicic Discontinuity (or "Moho"), the border between the crust and mantle. The resulting hole, drilled six miles into the ocean floor, was called a "Mohole." Samples of rock taken from the "Mohole" gave indirect proof of seafloor spreading, as well as evidence of locations for oil beneath the sea. This work continued through the decade and was aided immeasurably by the introduction of a technical wonder: the *Glomar Challenger,* a $12.6 million doughnut-shaped ship that could drill in water 20,000 feet deep and drill up to 2,500 feet beneath the ocean floor.

The beginning of the decade saw the *Trieste,* a bathyscaphe (manned vehicle designed to be submerged into deep seas), dive 37,000 feet deep into the Mariana Trench of the Pacific Ocean. The dive took four hours and forty-eight minutes, during which one-half hour was spent at the ocean's bottom. At this location, the bathyscaphe's hull withstood pressures of over 17,000 pounds per square inch. It was here that the crew was surprised to find forms of life where none had been thought possible, including a flat fish and several small shrimp.

Oceanic exploration in the 1960s also included several *Sealab* projects. *Sealabs* were underwater experimental chambers that were equipped for scientific study. Some scientists believed that people could live and work underwater for extended periods of time, and the *Sealab* project was an attempt to find out what problems such conditions would pose.

Sealab I submerged off Bermuda, a warm ocean area, in 1964. Four people stayed down for nine days at 192 feet. The next step was to experiment in a colder underwater region. For this purpose, *Sealab II* was employed. *Sealab II* was a 12-by-57 foot cylinder, and was made of steel. It contained life support and scientific research equipment, and was attached to its support barge on the surface by an "umbilical" cable, which also allowed closed-circuit telephone and television communications with the support barge. Supplies were lowered to *Sealab II* in pressurized containers. Three teams each spent fifteen days in the lab during the summer of 1965, living and working on the ocean floor off the coast of La Jolla, California. Former astronaut Scott Carpenter (1925–), leader of two of the missions, remained in *Sealab II* for a record thirty days. Because the craft rested at an angle during one of the missions, it won the nickname "The Tiltin' Hilton."

The *Sealab II* craft was lowered to a depth of 204 feet. Testing continued in *Sealab III,* which in 1969 plunged to depths of up to 600 feet off San Clemente Island, California. The mission of *Sealab III* was to test a system that would let divers exit a submarine, walk on the ocean floor, and retrieve objects. One diver died during a test, which effectively ended the *Sealab* project.

❖ **THE PILL: NEW CONTROL FOR WOMEN, AND A "MORAL CRISIS"**

The development and marketing of the birth control pill during the 1960s allowed women unprecedented control over their sexual behavior. Taken daily, birth control pills prevent the release of a fertilized egg from a

woman's ovaries, thus making it unlikely for her to become pregnant. Twelve different varieties of birth control pills were available, and women took them with increasing frequency. The first, Enovid, was approved by the U.S. Food and Drug Administration (FDA) in 1960. It was marketed by the Searle Pharmaceutical Company. By the end of 1961, 400,000 women were using Enovid; nearly 1.2 million were doing so a year later, and the number rose to 2.3 million by the end of 1963. In 1967, *Time* magazine reported that almost 20 percent of all American women who could conceive were using one form or another of oral contraception.

The availability of the pill raised a number of moral and health-related issues. In terms of health concerns, for example, the long-term effects of using birth control pills were unknown. Additionally, some critics argued that easy access to birth control was the same as condoning liberal sexual behavior. The nation's clergy were among the more vocal opponents of oral contraception. Catholic and Protestant leaders agreed that "there must be limitations and restrictions on the use of sex if we are to remain a civilized people." The concerns of clergy leaders did not necessarily affect the choices of women in their congregations, however. Reports during the decade showed that 20 percent of practicing Catholic women and nearly 30 percent of Protestant women had used the pill.

❖ THE SPACE PROGRAM: FROM ORBITING THE EARTH TO LANDING ON THE MOON

Probably the most well-known science story of the decade was the exploration of a "new frontier": space. As the decade began, a series of manned spacecraft orbited around Earth after being launched into space. Some of these forays were made by the United States, while others were achieved by the Soviet Union. Competition between the two superpowers to blast men into space and explore, and perhaps control the heavens was motivated by the cold war (the political, social, and economic battle between democracy and communism) then being waged between the two nations.

The United States named its first manned space flight program Project Mercury. Its space travelers were called astronauts. The initial Soviet program was named Project Vostok. Russian space travelers were called cosmonauts. The journeys into space by astronauts and cosmonauts alike were the decade's most highly publicized science and technology-related achievements.

In a January 1961 Project Mercury test flight, the National Aeronautics and Space Administration (NASA) launched into space a capsule containing a chimpanzee. The capsule traveled 5,000 miles per hour (mph), topping out at a height of 155 miles. Afterwards, the chimp was successfully recovered. However, the Russians one-upped the Americans by sending the first man into space. He was Yuri A. Gagarin (1934–1968), a cosmonaut who won the nickname "Columbus of the Cosmos." In April 1961, Gagarin was launched in the *Vostok 1* space vehicle. He reached a maximum altitude of 203 miles above Earth, and orbited the planet once during his 108-minute flight. "I see earth. It's so beautiful," were Gagarin's first words spoken from space. The success of his flight proved that a human being could withstand the rigors of liftoff from Earth, weightlessness while in space, and reentry back to Earth while still performing the manual operations necessary to spaceflight. Despite the competitive nature of space exploration, Gagarin later observed, "Circling the earth in the orbital spaceship, I marveled at the beauty of our planet. People of the world! Let us safeguard and enhance this beauty—not destroy it." Gagarin died in an air mishap in March 1968 while test-piloting a Russian MIG-15 jet.

A month after Gagarin's flight, U.S. Navy Commander Alan B. Shepard Jr. (1923–1998) became the first American in space. He was launched

On May 25, 1961, President John F. Kennedy (1917–1963), then in office for four months, delivered a "Special Message to the Congress on Urgent National Needs." In Kennedy's view, those "needs" involved the ability of the United States to keep pace with the Soviet Union in the then-escalating space race.

In this message, Kennedy declared, "First, I believe that this nation should commit itself to achieving the goal, before this decade is out, of landing a man on the moon and returning him safely to the Earth. No single space project in this period will be more impressive to mankind, or more important for the long-range exploration of space; and none will be so difficult or expensive to accomplish...."

into space in his Project Mercury capsule *Freedom 7*. Shepard's journey lasted all of 15 minutes and 28 seconds, during which he partially orbited Earth. He reached a maximum of 116 miles above Earth, and his top speed was 5,180 miles per hour.

The next human to soar into space was an American, Virgil "Gus" Grissom (1926–1967), whose journey came two month after Shepard's. Grissom's flight demonstrated the dangers of early space travel. Unlike the Soviets, who set down their craft on solid ground, Americans landed theirs in the ocean and recovered the astronaut and space capsule by ship. After his 15 minute and 37 second suborbital flight, the escape hatch of Grissom's spaceship, the *Liberty Bell 7*, prematurely blew open. The ship filled with water and sank, and Grissom had to swim to his rescuers.

In August 1961, cosmonaut Gherman S. Titov (1935–2000) became the first person to spend an entire day in space. His ship, *Vostok 2*, remained in space for 25 hours and 18 minutes, and orbited Earth seventeen times. The Soviets claimed that Titov felt fine after his flight. Later it became known that he was the first person to suffer from space sickness caused by the effects of weightlessness on the delicate balancing mechanisms of the inner ear. In February 1962, John H. Glenn Jr. (1921–) became the first American to orbit Earth. During its 4-hour, 55-minute flight, Glenn's spaceship, *Friendship 7*, made three orbits of Earth.

President Lyndon Johnson watches the first television transmission via a satellite that could transmit images all over the planet. Reproduced by permission of the Corbis Corporation.

All told, between 1961 and 1963, six Americans were blasted into space as part of Project Mercury. In 1961 and 1962, an equal number of Russians participated in the Project Vostok launches. The cosmonaut who flew the sixth and final flight, in June 1962, was also the first woman in space: Valentina V. Tereshkova (1937–). Despite suffering from severe space sickness, she was kept in orbit for almost three days.

In March 1965, the United States' space program began Project Gemini, the Project Mercury follow-up. Named after the "twins" sign in astrology, Project Gemini involved putting two astronauts in space at the same time. It was during the various Project Gemini missions that the Americans started to pull ahead of the Soviets in the space race. Edward H. White (1930–1967), one of the astronauts on board *Gemini 4*, launched in June 1965, became the first American to walk in space. The mission of *Gemini 7*, launched in December 1965, was space endurance. It remained in the skies for 13 days, 18 hours, and 35 minutes.

In 1967, the Soviets and the Americans both started new projects with the same goal: to land human beings on the moon. The Americans initiated

Project Apollo, while the Russians began Project Soyuz. In October 1968, *Apollo 7,* the first manned Apollo flight, began a 10-day, 20-hour mission. The highlight of the Apollo program and the culmination of America's space exploration during the decade was the first lunar landing, accomplished by *Apollo 11.* Takeoff was on July 16, 1969. On board were astronauts Neil A. Armstrong (1930–), Michael Collins (1930–), and Edwin "Buzz" Aldrin (1930–). The command module was named *Columbia,* and the lunar module was called *Eagle.* The two separated during lunar orbit, with Collins aboard the *Columbia* and Armstrong and Aldrin aboard the *Eagle.* At 9:18 P.M. on July 20, Americans reached the moon. Armstrong announced the arrival by declaring, "The *Eagle* has landed." Four hours later, he and Aldrin donned space suits. Armstrong was the first to come out of the module. On touching the moon's surface, he declared, "That's one small step for man, one giant leap for mankind." It was estimated that one-third of the world's population watched the event live on television.

The Apollo program also led to the first astronaut deaths of the U.S. space program. On January 27, 1967, Virgil "Gus" Grissom (1926– 1967), Edward H. White (1930–1967) and Roger Chaffee (1935–1967) were con-

Astronaut "Buzz" Aldrin was the first American to land on the moon in July 1969. **Photo courtesy of National Aeronautics and Space Administration (NASA).**

ducting a test in anticipation of the first three-person space flight. An electrical fire trapped the three astronauts inside the first Apollo/Saturn capsule while it was still on the launch pad. In the aftermath, the capsule's safety features were overhauled and significant changes were made in its construction and escape mechanisms. As the Apollo project progressed, the ill-fated mission was designated Apollo 1, in recognition of the crew members who lost their lives.

 For More Information

BOOKS

Bilger, Burkhard. *Global Warming (Earth at Risk)*. New York: Chelsea House, 1992.

Billings, Charlene W. *Lasers: The New Technology of Light*. New York: Facts on File, 1992.

Boon, Kevin Alexander. *The Human Genome Project: What Does Decoding DNA Mean for Us?* Berkeley Heights, NJ: Enslow Publishers, 2002.

Cole, Michael D. *John Glenn: Astronaut and Senator*. Rev. ed. Berkeley Heights, NJ: Enslow Publishers, 2000. (revised)

Couper, Heather, and Nigel Henbest. *Big Bang: The Story of the Universe*. New York: DK Publishing, 1996.

Couper, Heather, and Nigel Henbest. *DK Space Encyclopedia*. New York: DK Publishing, 1999.

Couper, Heather, and Nigel Henbest. *The Guide to the Galaxy*. New York and Cambridge, England: Cambridge University Press, 1994.

Couper, Heather, and Nigel Henbest. *How the Universe Works*. Pleasantville, NY: Reader's Digest Association, 1994.

Couper, Heather, and Nigel Henbest. *New Worlds: In Search of the Planets*. Reading, MA: Addison-Wesley, 1985.

Dudzinski, Kathleen. *Meeting Dolphins: My Adventures in the Sea*. Washington, DC: National Geographic Society, 2000.

Dukert, Joseph M. *Nuclear Ships of the World*. New York: Coward, McCann & Geoghegan, 1973.

Dyson, Marianne J. *Space Station Science: Life in Free Fall*. New York: Scholastic Trade, 1999.

Engelbert, Phyllis, ed. *Astronomy & Space: From the Big Bang to the Big Crunch*. Detroit: U•X•L, 1996.

Fridell, Ron. *Global Warming*. New York: Franklin Watts, 2002.

Gardner, Robert. *Health Science Projects About Heredity*. Berkeley Heights, NJ: Enslow Publishers, 2001.

Green, Robert. *John Glenn: Astronaut and U.S. Senator.* Chicago: Ferguson Publishing, 2001.

Haley, James, ed. *Global Warming: Opposing Viewpoints.* San Diego, CA: Greenhaven Press, 2002.

Johnson, Rebecca L. *The Greenhouse Effect: Life on a Warmer Planet.* Minneapolis: Lerner Publications, 1993.

Kramer, Barbara. *Neil Armstrong: The First Man on the Moon.* Springfield, NJ: Enslow Publishers, 1997.

Lambert, Lisa A. *The Leakeys.* Vero Beach, FL: Roarke Publishers, 1993.

Malatesta, Anne, and Ronald Friedland. *The White Kikuya: Louis S.B. Leakey.* New York: McGraw-Hill, 1978.

Nardo, Don. *Lasers: Humanity's Magic Light.* San Diego, CA: Lucent Books, 1990.

Northrup, Mary. *American Computer Pioneers.* Springfield, NJ: Enslow Publishers, 1998.

Pogue, William R. *How Do You Go to the Bathroom in Space?* New York: Tom Doherty Associates, 1999. (revised)

Poynter, Margaret. *The Leakeys: Uncovering the Origins of Humankind.* Springfield, NJ: Enslow Publishers, 1997.

Roleff, Tamara, ed. *Global Warming: Opposing Viewpoints.* San Diego, CA: Greenhaven Press, 1997.

Sharpe, Mitchell R. *"It Is I, Sea Gull": Valentina Tereshkova, First Woman in Space.* New York: Crowell, 1975.

Smith, Howard E. *Daring the Unknown: A History of NASA.* San Diego, CA: Harcourt Brace Jovanovich, 1987.

Spangenburg, Ray, and Diane K. Moser. *Living and Working in Space.* New York: Facts on File, 1989.

Spangenburg, Ray, and Diane K. Moser. *Opening the Space Frontier.* New York: Facts on File, 1989.

Spangenburg, Ray, and Diane K. Moser. *Space Exploration: Exploring the Reaches of the Solar System.* New York: Facts on File, 1990.

Spangenburg, Ray, and Kit Moser. *Artificial Satellites.* New York: Franklin Watts, 2001.

Spangenburg, Ray, and Kit Moser. *History of NASA.* New York: Franklin Watts, 2000.

Spangenburg, Ray, and Kit Moser. *Project Apollo.* New York: Franklin Watts, 2001.

Spangenburg, Ray, and Kit Moser. *Project Gemini.* New York: Franklin Watts, 2001.

Spangenburg, Ray, and Kit Moser. *Project Mercury.* New York: Franklin Watts, 2001.

Streissguth, Tom. *John Glenn.* Minneapolis: Lerner Publications, 1999.

Stwertka, Albert, and Eve Stwertka. *Physics: From Newton to the Big Bang.* New York: Franklin Watts, 1986.

Tesar, Jenny. *Global Warming.* New York: Facts on File, 1991.

Thro, Ellen. *Robotics: The Marriage of Computers and Machines.* New York, Facts on File, 1993.

Tilton, Rafael. *John Glenn (The Importance Of).* San Diego, CA: Lucent Books, 2001.

Vogt, Gregory. *Apollo and the Moon Landing.* Brookfield, CT: Millbrook Press, 1991.

Vogt, Gregory. *John Glenn's Return to Space.* Brookfield, CT: Millbrook Press, 2000.

Vogt, Gregory. *The Solar System: Facts and Exploration.* New York: Twenty-First Century Books, 1995.

Vogt, Gregory. *The Space Shuttle: Missions in Space.* Brookfield, CT: Millbrook Press, 1991.

Vogt, Gregory. *A Twenty-Fifth Anniversary Album of NASA.* New York: Franklin Watts, 1983.

Weiss, Malcolm E. *Man Explores the Sea.* New York: J. Messner, 1969.

Willis, Delta. *The Leakey Family: Leaders in the Search for Human Origins.* New York: Facts on File, 1992.

WEB SITES

Biographies: Louis Leakey. http://www.talkorigins.org/faqs/homs/lleakey.html (accessed on August 6, 2002).

Greatest Space Events of the 20th Century: The 60s. http://www.space.com/news/spacehistory/greatest_space_events_1960s.html (accessed on August 6, 2002).

Planned Parenthood Federation of America—1960s. http://member.planned parenthood.org/site/PageServer?pagename=1960s (accessed on August 6, 2002).

chapter eight *Sports*

1960: **October 14** Bill Mazeroski hits a ninth-inning home run to break a 9 to 9 tie, leading the Pittsburgh Pirates to a Game 7 World Series victory over the New York Yankees.

1960: **October 16** The National League (NL) adds two new franchises, the New York Mets and Houston Colt .45s, which begin play in 1962.

1960: **October 27** The American League (AL) adds two new franchises, the Los Angeles Angels and Washington Senators, which begin play in 1961; the Senators become the present-day Minnesota Twins.

1961: **January 2** Seventeen-year-old Bobby Fischer wins his fourth consecutive U.S. chess championship.

1961: **February 15** The entire U.S. figure-skating team is killed in a plane crash while traveling to the world championships in Prague, Czechoslovakia.

1961: **October 1** Roger Maris hits his sixty-first home run, breaking the record held by Babe Ruth since 1927.

1962: **February 10** Jim Beatty becomes the first person to run the mile indoors in under four minutes.

1962: **July 31** The National League rebuffs a bid by baseball commissioner Ford Frick to begin interleague play in 1963.

1963: **April 13** Cincinnati Reds rookie Pete Rose smacks his first major league hit.

1964: **February 25** Cassius Clay, who would change his name to Muhammed Ali a month later, wins the heavyweight boxing crown from Sonny Liston.

1964: **July 12** The Major League Baseball Players Association (MLBPA), America's first effective sports union, is formed.

1964: **September 1** The San Francisco Giants' Masanori Murakami becomes the first Japanese player to appear in the major leagues.

1965: **September 25** Fifty-nine-year-old baseball legend Satchel Paige pitches three scoreless innings for the Kansas City Athletic's.

1966: **February 27** Seventeen-year-old Peggy Fleming, three-time U.S. champion, wins the world figure-skating championship.

1966: **March 12** Bobby Hull becomes the first National Hockey League (NHL) player to score fifty goals in a season.

1966: **March 19** Highly favored all-white Kentucky is upset in the National Collegiate Athletic Association (NCAA) basketball finals by all-black Texas Western.

1966: **April 11** Emmett Ashford becomes major league baseball's first black umpire.

1966: **April 11** Jack Nicklaus becomes the first golfer to win two straight Masters titles.

1966: **June 8** A merger between the established National Football League (NFL) and the upstart American Football League (AFL) is announced. It will go into effect in 1970.

1966: **July 17** Nineteen-year-old Jim Ryun sets a world record of 3:51.3 in the mile.

1966: **November 19** In what might be the decade's greatest college football game, Notre Dame and the University of Michigan play to a 10 to 10 tie.

1967: **January 15** The Green Bay Packers wallop the Kansas City Chiefs, 35 to 10, in the first AFL-NFL championship game.

1967: **May 2** The Toronto Maple Leafs win their fourth Stanley Cup of the 1960s.

1967: **June 20** Muhammad Ali is stripped of his title as heavyweight boxing champion for refusing military service, both on religious grounds and to protest continued military action in Vietnam.

1967: **July–August** The United States wins 225 of the 537 medals awarded to twenty-seven nations in the Pan-American games.

1968: **May 4** Dancer's Image is disqualified as winner of the Kentucky Derby after a urine test shows signs of a painkiller.

1968: **September 9** Arthur Ashe becomes the first African American to win the U.S. Open Tennis Tournament.

1969: **January 12** The New York Jets stun the Baltimore Colts, 16 to 7, in Super Bowl III.

1969: **May 4** The Montreal Canadiens win their fifth Stanley Cup of the 1960s.

1969: **May 5** The Boston Celtics win the National Basketball Association (NBA) championship for the eleventh time in thirteen years.

1969: **October 16** The "Miracle Mets" win the World Series.

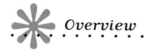

Overview

During the 1960s, baseball reigned as America's most cherished sport. Dozens of hall-of-fame-caliber ballplayers thrilled fans with on-field heroics during the decade. The decade began with the assault by Roger Maris on one of baseball's sacred records: the sixty home runs hit by the legendary Babe Ruth during the 1927 season. It ended with the World Series triumph of the "Miracle" New York Mets.

At the same time, other professional sports vied for the public's attention. Professional football began to infringe on baseball's status as America's national pastime. The Super Bowl, which first pitted the champions of the more established National Football League (NFL) and the upstart American Football League (AFL), did much to boost the sport's status. The third Super Bowl, in which the AFL's New York Jets and quarterback Joe Namath upset the heavily favored NFL's Baltimore Colts, proved a pivotal moment in the growth of pro football. In the world of pro basketball, the Boston Celtics thoroughly dominated the National Basketball Association (NBA). But the hoop game still lagged behind baseball and football among major sports. Furthermore, the status of the NBA as the premier basketball entity was threatened by a new, upstart league, the American Basketball Association (ABA). Especially in small town and rural America, auto racing—sponsored by both the National Association of Stock Car Auto Racing (NASCAR) and United States Auto Club (USAC)—emerged as a popular spectator sport.

College football and basketball were wildly popular. While television allowed the best teams to enjoy nationwide acclaim, hundreds of thousands of fans still packed college stadiums and basketball arenas to cheer on their favorite teams. The University of Southern California (UCLA) basketball team reeled off eighty-eight straight victories; during the decade's football seasons, a number of teams also completed perfect (or near-perfect) records.

Three separate summer and winter Olympic games were held during the decade. While records were set and medals were won at each, international and national politics overshadowed the games. Of all the decade's sports personalities, none mixed politics, athletics, and controversy more than Muhammad Ali. Ali, born Cassius Marcellus Clay, started the decade as a brash young boxer who won Olympic gold in 1960. He took the heavyweight title in 1964, but eventually lost it to an opponent outside the ring. In 1967, as the Vietnam War was escalating, he refused induction into the U.S. military on the basis of being a conscientious objector (a person who is against armed conflict because he or she believes it is wrong to kill for any reason). He had joined the Nation of Islam (Black Muslims) and changed his name from Clay to Ali. Furthermore, he stated that he would not fight in Southeast Asia because he "ain't got no quarrel with the Viet Cong." At the time, this was a bold, incendiary statement from such a prominent figure in or out of the sporting world, let alone one who was African American. Ali summarily was stripped of his title and banned from boxing.

Muhammad Ali (1942–) Boxer Muhammad Ali was one of the decade's most charismatic, controversial personalities. In 1964, he became heavyweight champ upon beating Sonny Liston (1932–1970). He knocked out Liston in a rematch and defeated a string of contenders. Then in 1967 Clay, who had earlier become a Black Muslim and changed his name to Muhammad Ali, was stripped of his title and banned from fighting for refusing induction into the U.S. military, claiming conscientious objector status. He regained the crown in 1974, when he knocked out George Foreman (1949–). *Photo reproduced by permission of the Corbis Corporation.*

Jim Brown (1936–) Jim Brown was one of the most dominant NFL players of the 1960s. A fullback for the Cleveland Browns, he played in the league for only nine seasons, beginning in 1957, but he led the NFL in rushing eight times. He amassed 12,312 yards, rushed for 106 touchdowns, and scored 756 points. Brown was named Rookie of the Year in 1957, and the league's Most Valuable Player (MVP) the following season and in 1965. He rushed for more than 100 yards in 58 games, and reached 200 on four occasions.

Roberto Clemente (1934–1972) Roberto Clemente was the first Hispanic ballplayer elected to the Baseball Hall of Fame. But during his lifetime, he was underappreciated by America's baseball fans and his contemporaries. He won four National League batting titles and twelve straight Gold Gloves for his fielding. One reason was because of prejudice against Hispanic ballplayers. On the final day of the 1972 season, Clemente smacked his three-thousandth major league hit. On New Year's Eve 1972, he was killed in a plane crash while flying relief supplies to Nicaraguan earthquake victims. *Photo reproduced by permission of the Corbis Corporation.*

Sandy Koufax (1935–) Many hard-throwing young pitchers show much promise, but quickly fizzle in their major league careers. Not so Sandy Koufax. After a rocky start in the mid-1950s, he matured and became one of the all-time great hurlers. Between 1962 and 1966, Koufax pitched four no-hitters (including a perfect game), earned five earned run average titles, and won three Cy Young Awards and one MVP title. After winning 27 games in 1966, an arthritic elbow caused Koufax to retire, at the age of 30. *Photo reproduced by permission of the Corbis Corporation.*

Vince Lombardi (1913–1970) Long a losing team, the Green Bay Packers hired New York Giants assistant Vince Lombardi as head coach in 1959. It was a smart move. Lombardi was a tough, bullying coach who goaded top performances out of his players. He remained with the team for nine seasons, leaving with a record of 89 and 24 and 2, six conference titles, five NFL championships, and two Super Bowl victories. Eleven of Lombardi's Packers made it to the Football Hall of Fame. *Photo reproduced by permission of Archive Photos, Inc.*

Al Oerter (1936–) During the 1960s Al Oerter excelled at discus throwing. He earned four world records, as well as four Olympic gold medals and was the first man to ever throw the discus more than 200 feet. Oerter participated in the 1956 Olympic games where he won his first gold medal. In 1957 Oerter was involved in a serious automobile accident that almost took his life. Although he regained his strength, he was never able to compete again without pain. Oerter won two more medals in the 1960 and 1964 Olympics. During the 1968 Olympics, Oerter threw the discus 212 feet, 6 inches to win his fourth gold medal. *Photo reproduced by permission of AP/Wide World Photos.*

Frank Robinson (1935–) Frank Robinson broke into the major leagues in 1956 and for the next decade starred for the Cincinnati Reds. The Reds then believed his career was on the downside, so they traded him to Baltimore. The Reds were mistaken, however. Not only did Robinson lead the Orioles to the World Championship in 1966, but he won the Triple Crown with 49 homeruns, 122 runs batted in, and a .316 batting average. Robinson was the first player to win MVP awards in both the American and National leagues, and he finished his career with 586 homeruns. *Photo reproduced by permission of Archive Photos, Inc.*

Bill Russell (1934–) When Bill Russell signed with the Boston Celtics in 1957, the team became a dominant force within the NBA during the 1960s. The Celtics won their first championship during Russell's rookie year, and in the next twelve years they won ten times more. Russell was named league MVP five times during those years. When Red Auderbach retired as the Celtics' coach in 1967, he named Russell to succeed him. He was the first black man in history to coach a major league professional team. Russell retired at the start of the 1970 season. *Photo reproduced by permission of the Corbis Corporation.*

◆◆◆ *Topics in the News* •••••••••••••••••••••••••

❖ **AUTO RACING: NASCAR AND USAC**

By the 1960s, the National Association of Stock Car Auto Racing (NASCAR), founded in 1947, had evolved into a well-organized professional racing circuit. While the sport had national appeal (albeit mostly in the country's rural areas), NASCAR was based in the South and most of its star drivers and hard-core fans were Southern. At the end of the decade, NASCAR membership comprised over 20,000 race supporters and sponsors; the association sanctioned over fifty races annually.

The stock cars NASCAR drivers race are radically modified versions of regular passenger automobiles. However, some drivers prefer cars that are expressly designed for sport and are undrivable on public roads. Such cars are the ones that compete in the Indianapolis 500, the most renowned auto race. Since 1911, the Indy 500 has been held each May at the Indianapolis Motor Speedway; it consists of two hundred laps around a 2.5-mile track. In 1955, the United States Auto Club (USAC) was founded as the governing body for Indy-type racers. Each year through the 1960s and beyond, the USAC sponsored a full slate of races and named an annual racing champion. It also marketed the Indy 500 as the jewel of car races.

Richard Petty (1937–) was the era's preeminent stock car racer. In 1967, he won twenty-seven of forty-eight NASCAR events, finishing in the top five in all except ten. Concurrently, Indy-style racers began driving new kinds of cars with new kinds of engines, which allowed them to zoom across racetracks. Car owner Andy Granatelli (1923–) even introduced a turbine engine that some said should have been outlawed because it was more suitable for an airplane than a racecar! The decade's most eminent USAC racer was A. J. Foyt (1935–), who entered his first Indy 500 in 1958 and established a record for making thirty-five consecutive starts. Foyt won three Indy 500s during the decade (in 1961, 1964, and 1967) and five USAC championships (in 1960, 1961, 1963, 1964, and 1967).

Auto racing was, and remains, a dangerous and sometimes deadly sport. At the 1964 World 600 stock car race, held at the Charlotte Motor Speedway, "Fireball" Roberts (1931–1964) was seriously injured when his car crashed and became engulfed in flames. He was burned over 40 percent of his body; doctors worked to save him, pumping 123 pints of blood into him, during the thirty-nine days before he died. Roberts (whose given name was Glenn) was one of the era's top racers.

OPPOSITE PAGE
*The Indianapolis 500 was marketed as the jewel of car races. **Reproduced by permission of the Corbis Corporation.***

In 1964 and 1965, drivers Jim Pardue, Eddie Sachs, Joe Weatherly, Billy Wade, Buren Skeen, and Harold Kite were all killed in races or during tire tests. They were neither the first nor the last to die while competing in auto races.

Indianapolis 500 Winners

Year	Driver
1960	Jim Rathmann
1961	A. J. Foyt
1962	Rodger Ward
1963	Parnelli Jones
1964	A. J. Foyt
1965	Jim Clark
1966	Graham Hill
1967	A. J. Foyt
1968	Bobby Unser
1969	Mario Andretti

❖ BASEBALL: FROM MARIS TO A "MIRACLE"

In 1927, Babe Ruth (1895–1948), the legendary Sultan of Swat, belted sixty home runs. It was a record revered by baseball fans and sportswriters. Then in 1961, another New York Yankee, Roger Maris (1934–1985), cracked sixty-one.

At the time, the mark was controversial. Who was this Maris, anyway? Fans had not rallied behind Roger Maris, the player who had competed with a different, favored Yankee, Mickey Mantle (1931–1995), to best the record. Mantle, unlike Maris, had been a Bronx Bomber for a decade and was already acknowledged as a New York icon. During the season, Mantle and Maris swatted homer after homer, but in the end Mantle finished the season with only fifty-four four-base hits.

Although Maris had hit sixty-one homers, the validity of his record was contested. During the 1961 season, the American League (AL) had expanded from eight teams to ten and eight games had been added to the standard 154-game schedule. Because Maris did not break Ruth's mark during the first 154 contests, Baseball Commissioner Ford Frick (1894–1978) ruled that Ruth's name still would appear in the record books; Maris's would, too, but with an asterisk. Meanwhile, the Yankees, a powerhouse team throughout the previous decade, maintained their win-

Major League Baseball World Series Champions

Year	Team
1960	Pittsburgh Pirates
1961	New York Yankees
1962	New York Yankees
1963	Los Angeles Dodgers
1964	St. Louis Cardinals
1965	Los Angeles Dodgers
1966	Baltimore Orioles
1967	St. Louis Cardinals
1968	Detroit Tigers
1969	New York Mets

ning ways. During the decade's first five years, they competed in every World Series. Then in 1965, they slipped to sixth place. The following season, they wound up last in the AL.

Meanwhile, a new generation of baseball greats won stardom. A short list includes Pete Rose, Carl Yastrzemski, Bob Gibson, Jim Palmer, Frank Howard, Orlando Cepeda, Willie McCovey, Juan Marichal, Lou Brock, Tony Oliva, Ron Santo, Dave McNally, Richie (later Dick) Allen, Tom Seaver, Ferguson Jenkins, Catfish Hunter, Luis Tiant, Tony Perez, and Reggie Jackson. Nineteen-sixty-eight was a noteworthy year for baseball, in that pitchers dominated hitters like never before. Among hurlers, St. Louis Cardinal hall-of-famer Bob Gibson (1935–) finished the season with a microscopic 1.12 earned run average (ERA), while pitcher Denny McLain (1944–) of the Detroit Tigers won thirty-one games. Among hitters, Boston Red Sox outfielder Carl Yastrzemski (1939–) won the 1968 AL batting championship with a lowly .301 average, the puniest in history. The next-best hitter, Danny Cater (1940–), averaged .290. Despite this emphasis on pitching, the decade's second half saw two AL Triple Crown winners. In 1966, Frank Robinson (1935–) of the Baltimore Orioles led in batting average (.316), runs batted in (122), and home runs (49). The following season, the winner Yastrzemski totaled .326, 121, and 44.

Baseball Union

July 12, 1964 is one of the most significant days in baseball history. On that date, the Major League Baseball Players' Association (MLBPA) was formed. At the time, ballplayers were bound to the clubs that owned their contracts. They could not declare themselves free agents and sign with other teams. The newly formed MLBPA was the first genuinely effective sports union in the United States. In subsequent decades, it won for its members the right to work for any employer who wanted to hire them, just like other American workers.

Through the 1961 season, the National League (NL) and the American League (AL) were made up of eight teams each. At the end of each season, the two first-place teams competed in the World Series. However, in 1961, the AL expanded by two teams, adding the Los Angeles Angels and Washington Senators; the team previously known as the Senators became the Minnesota Twins. Then in 1962, the NL added the New York Mets and Houston Colt .45s. Seven years later, four expansion teams began play, two (the Montreal Expos and San Diego Padres) in the NL and two (the Kansas City Royals and Seattle Pilots) in the AL. After one season, the Pilots relocated to the Midwest, becoming the Milwaukee Brewers. The decade saw two other team relocations. Back in the 1950s, the Boston Braves moved to Milwaukee and the Philadelphia Athletics shifted to Kansas City. In 1966, the Braves headed south to Atlanta; two years later, the A's headed west to Oakland. Finally, starting in 1969, each league was split into two divisions, an Eastern and Western. The first-place teams competed in a playoff round, with the winner going on to the World Series.

The New York Mets were the decade's most colorful, unpredictable ballclub. During its inaugural season, the Mets compiled a 40 and 120 record, the worst ever for a team during the twentieth century. However, New Yorkers did not mind. They had been deprived of NL baseball since the Brooklyn Dodgers and New York Giants headed west at the end of the 1957 season and were overjoyed by the Mets' mere presence, and charmed by the team's ineptitude.

Incredibly, by the end of the decade, the team evolved into world champions. In 1969, the "Miracle Mets" won the NL East, then swept the

NCAA Division I Men's Basketball Champions

1960:	Ohio State
1961:	Cincinnati
1962:	Cincinnati
1963:	Loyola (Illinois)
1964:	UCLA
1965:	UCLA
1966:	Texas Western (Texas-El Paso)
1967:	UCLA
1968:	UCLA
1969:	UCLA

Atlanta Braves in the playoffs, and took four of five games against the Baltimore Orioles in the World Series.

❖ COLLEGE BASKETBALL: UCLA DOMINANCE

In the early 1950s, a point-shaving scandal rocked the world of college basketball. By the following decade, the scandal was becoming a dim memory as the sport enjoyed steadily increasing popularity.

The University of Cincinnati won National Collegiate Athletic Association (NCAA) titles in 1961 and 1962. However, the reigning college team of the 1960s and 1970s played on the West Coast. Under legendary coach John Wooden (1910–), the University of California at Los Angeles (UCLA) won NCAA titles in 1964 and 1965. After Texas Western emerged victorious in 1966, the Bruins earned consecutive championships from 1967 to 1973. It won one last time, in 1975, at which point Wooden retired from coaching. Among his stars were Lew Alcindor (later known as Kareem Abdul-Jabbar), Gail Goodrich, Sidney Wicks, Mike Warren, Walt Hazzard, and Bill Walton.

At one point, Wooden led the team to an NCAA-record eighty-eight consecutive victories over three seasons. During his twenty-three years as UCLA's coach, Wooden's teams won over 80 percent of their games. Decades earlier, he had been a schoolboy star in his home state of Indiana and later as a guard playing at Purdue. Wooden became the first man ever elected to the Basketball Hall of Fame as both player and coach.

Despite UCLA's run, the victory by Texas Western arguably was the one game that most changed college basketball. In 1966, many teams, particularly those in the South, still were segregated. One was the Kentucky Wildcats, coached by Adolph Rupp (1901–1977). Although Rupp had won four national championships, he had never allowed a black player on his team. That year, Kentucky was undefeated going into the NCAA final. Its opponent was Texas Western, a small, independent school that never had vied for a sports title of any kind. In addition, its players were black. They played what was called "black basketball": a fast, flashy game that featured plenty of running and jumping. Texas Western led throughout, and came away with the championship by beating Rupp and Kentucky, 72 to 65. The victory was the beginning of the end for segregation in college basketball.

❖ GROWTH OF PROFESSIONAL BASKETBALL

At the dawn of the 1960s, the National Basketball Association (NBA) was an eight-team league, separated into two divisions. The decade saw many changes within the basic league structure, highlighted by the addition of the first expansion teams since the league was founded more than a decade earlier.

The decade began with a franchise switch, as the Minneapolis Lakers moved to Los Angeles. In 1961, the league added its initial expansion team, the Chicago Packers. The following year, the Packers were renamed the Zephyrs and the Philadelphia Warriors headed west to San Francisco. In 1963, the Chicago franchise moved to Baltimore and was renamed the Bullets, while the Syracuse Nationals became the Philadelphia 76ers. Then in 1966, a second expansion team was added, also in Chicago, named the Bulls. The following year, two more teams were added: the San Diego Rockets and Seattle SuperSonics. They were followed in 1968 by the Milwaukee Bucks and Phoenix Suns. Meanwhile, the St. Louis Hawks moved to Atlanta.

The decade saw its share of celebrated teams, players, and games. Beginning in 1959, the Boston Celtics, coached by Arnold "Red" Auerbach (1917–), earned an incredible eight straight NBA titles. The Celtics were dominated by two hall-of-famers: Bill Russell (1934–), a rugged center who was fabled as a shot-blocker; and Bob Cousy (1928–), a sure-handed guard. Russell in particular built up a rivalry with another all-time-great NBA big man: Wilt Chamberlain (1936–1999). Some of the top teams in league history played during the 1960s. The 1964 and 1965 Boston Celtics ended the regular season at 62 and 18, setting a record for most victories.

Bill Russell, John Havlicek, Tom Heinsohn, Sam Jones, and Tom Sanders were the team's stars. In one of the all-time-great playoff games, the Celtics bested the Philadelphia 76ers 110 to 109 in Game 7 of the Eastern Division Finals. Their 4 to 1 pounding of the Los Angeles Lakers in the NBA finals seemed anticlimactic. Boston emerged with its seventh consecutive championship.

The 1966 and 1967 Philadelphia 76ers began the season with a 46 and 4 mark. The team finished at 68 and 13, setting yet another regular season victory record. Chamberlain, Hal Greer, Billy Cunningham, and Chet Walker sparked the team, which beat Boston 4 to 1 in the Eastern Division Finals, and insured that the Celtics would not win a ninth-straight NBA title. The 76ers topped the San Francisco Warriors, 4 to 2, for the championship. The 1969 and 1970 New York Knicks did not have the all-time best regular season record; they finished at 60 and 22. However, this team was celebrated for its intelligent, pass-oriented play. Six top players sparked the Knicks: Willis Reed, Walt Frazier, Dave DeBusschere, Bill Bradley, Dick Barnett, and Cazzie Russell. They captured the franchise's first NBA championship by beating the Lakers 4 to 3 in the league finals. Team captain Reed sat out Game 6 with a torn leg muscle. Before the deciding contest, he inspired teammates and fans by hobbling onto the Madison Square Garden court. Reed started the game, and even made the Knicks' first two baskets. His team won, 113 to 99.

At the start of the 1967 and 1968 basketball season, a newly formed basketball league challenged the NBA: The American Basketball Association (ABA).

By the mid-1960s the NBA was expanding, but not quickly enough for community leaders in cities that lacked league franchises. Furthermore, entry fees for new franchises were high. Businessmen in cities from Louisville and New Orleans to Oakland and Anaheim were convinced their towns could support pro basketball. So they banded together and formed the ABA. In its first season, five teams played in the Eastern Division: the Indiana Pacers, Kentucky Colonels, Minnesota Muskies, New Jersey Americans, and Pittsburgh Pipers. Six teams made up the Western Division: the Anaheim Amigos, Dallas Chaparrals, Denver Rockets, Houston Mavericks, New Orleans Buccaneers, and Oakland Oaks.

While the first ABA teams were not as good as their NBA rivals, individual players easily could have competed in the older league. George Mikan (1924–), an NBA star of the 1950s, became the first ABA commissioner. He concocted the idea of coloring the official league ball red, white, and blue. Not only would these shades add a patriotic flair to the game, but they would stand out on the court and on television.

NBA Champions

1959–60:	Boston Celtics
1960–61:	Boston Celtics
1961–62:	Boston Celtics
1962–63:	Boston Celtics
1963–64:	Boston Celtics
1964–65:	Boston Celtics
1965–66:	Boston Celtics
1966–67:	Philadelphia 76ers
1967–68:	Boston Celtics
1968–69:	Boston Celtics
1969–70:	New York Knicks

The ABA lasted nine seasons, through 1975 and 1976. At that time, four of its teams joined the NBA: Indiana Pacers, New York Nets, San Antonio Spurs, and Denver Nuggets.

❖ COLLEGE FOOTBALL: GREAT TEAMS, GREAT PLAYERS

The 1960s saw an array of college football legends. One of the greatest was O. J. Simpson (1947–), who later became notorious as the defendant in one of the twentieth century's most controversial murder cases. During the 1967 season, Simpson led the University of Southern California (USC) with 3,187 rushing yards and 34 touchdowns. In 1968, he set an NCAA record with 334 carries and 1,654 yards, and won the Heisman Trophy. Noted his coach, John McKay (1923–), "Simpson was not only the greatest player I ever had—he was the greatest player anyone ever had."

Television had no small role in transforming players like Simpson into national heroes. And TV also allowed individual teams to win national followings. Notre Dame, Navy, Michigan State, Ohio State, Alabama, and USC were among the decade's glamour teams. However, television did not keep fans away from cheering on their favorite teams in person. During the 1962 season, for example, 22,337,094 fans attended college games.

The decade saw several teams compile perfect or near-perfect win-loss records. Yale (1960), New Mexico (1960), USC (1962), the University of

1960:	Minnesota
1961:	Alabama
1962:	University of Southern California
1963:	Texas
1964:	Alabama
1965:	Alabama/Michigan State
1966:	Notre Dame
1967:	University of Southern California
1968:	Ohio State
1969:	Texas

Texas (1963 and 1969), Alabama (1964), Arkansas (1964), Ohio State (1968), and Penn State (1968 and 1969) all completed undefeated seasons. In 1967, Simpson's USC Trojans finished 10 and 1, as had the Michigan State Spartans in 1965. In 1966, Notre Dame and Michigan each posted 9 and 0 and 1 records. That one tie came in a game in which they opposed each other; the Fighting Irish and Spartans were an equal match, and the game ended with the score 10 to 10. Many fans and observers of the sport declared it the decade's greatest college football game.

❖ EXPANSION AND RIVALRY IN PROFESSIONAL FOOTBALL

In 1958, the National Football League (NFL) came to maturity when the Baltimore Colts topped the New York Giants 23 to 17 in overtime, in one of the most thrilling and significant games in league history. However, the following decade saw the beginning of a period of unparalleled growth for the league. The individual most responsible was neither a player nor a coach. In 1960, Pete Rozelle (1926–1996) became NFL commissioner. He held the post for the next three decades. Under Rozelle's stewardship, league attendance skyrocketed. The NFL negotiated lucrative deals with television networks, and marketed itself as a unified professional sports entity.

Just as Rozelle came into office, a new eight-team pro football league was formed. It was named the American Football League (AFL), and was determined to compete with the NFL. The league suffered growing pains: its franchises in Los Angeles and New York drew small crowds, with football fans preferring to follow the exploits of the city's NFL teams. After its first season, the division-winning Los Angeles Chargers headed south to San Diego because the team could not draw a fan base against the city's NFL team, the Rams. The Boston Patriots called four different stadiums home during their first eleven years; and the home fields of the Oakland and Houston franchises were high-school stadiums. However, the AFL competed with the older league for college players. Its most significant acquisition came in 1965, when the New York Jets signed Alabama star quarterback Joe Namath (1943–) to a then-astounding $437,000 contract. By then, the AFL had begun developing its own roster of stars. Ex-NFL quarterback George Blanda (1927–) led the Houston Oilers to the first two AFL titles and played for another fifteen years; his pro career lasted twenty-six seasons. Jack Kemp (1935–) became one of the league's top quarterbacks, leading the Buffalo Bills to two titles. Wide receivers Don Maynard (1935–) of the New York Titans (who in 1963 became the Jets) and Lance Alworth (1940–) of San Diego became hall-of-famers in the AFL. Buffalo Bills fullback Cookie Gilchrist (1935–) became the AFL's first 1,000-yard rusher. Two years after signing with the Jets, Namath was the first quarterback to pass for 4,000 yards in a season.

Joe Namath was one of the best and highest-paid football players of the 1960s. Reproduced by permission of AP/Wide World Photos.

In 1966, peace came to pro football when the two leagues merged. At first they continued as separate leagues, with their top teams competing in a championship game that came to be known as the Super Bowl. The Green Bay Packers won the first two meetings, easily beating the Kansas City Chiefs, 35 to 20, and the Oakland Raiders, 33 to 14. The third go-round featured the New York Jets against the heavily favored Baltimore Colts. Before the game, Namath, the Jets quarterback, brashly forecast victory. Then, he set about leading his team to a surprise 16 to 7 win. This triumph not only validated the NFL-AFL union, but established the Super Bowl as an important sporting event and added to the success and status of professional football.

The NFL-AFL rivalry aside, one team easily dominated professional football during the 1960s: the Green Bay Packers. In addition to those first

1966:	Green Bay Packers
1967:	Green Bay Packers
1968:	New York Jets
1969:	Kansas City Chiefs

two Super Bowl victories, the Packers won six conference titles and five NFL championships. Early in the decade, the Packers' primary rivals were the New York Giants. Yet their most dramatic victory during the decade came in the 1967 NFL championship game, a gritty clash that came to be known as the "Ice Bowl" because, at kickoff, the temperature was minus 13 degrees Fahrenheit, with a 15-mile-per-hour wind. With thirteen seconds left, Bart Starr (1934–) scored on a quarterback sneak, resulting in a 21 to 17 Packers victory.

❖ OLYMPICS: PERFORMANCE AND POLITICS

Three Summer Olympics were held during the decade: in 1960 (Rome), 1964 (Tokyo), and 1968 (Mexico City). In 1960, Rafer Johnson (1935–) won the decathlon with a stunning victory in the 10,000-meter race. Wilma Rudolph (1940–1994) put on a one-woman track-and-field show, winning gold in the 100-meter and 200-meter events and as anchor for the 400-meter relay. In 1964, swimmer Don Schollander (1946–) won four gold medals. Bob Hayes (1942–) earned the title "world's fastest human" with a ten-second flat time in the 100-meter race. In 1968, Bob Beamon (1946–) set a world record in the long jump of 8.9 meters. Dick Fosbury (1947–) introduced a new style of high jumping, called the "Fosbury Flop," that revolutionized the sport. Perhaps the era's top U.S. Olympic champion was Al Oerter (1936–), who won gold medals in the discus throw in four consecutive games beginning in 1956. In 1964, Oerter became the first man ever to throw the discus more than 200 feet.

However, the Olympics primarily served as a political forum, despite its stated purpose of promoting international harmony. The cold war, pitting West (in particular, the United States) against East (in particular, the Soviet Union), had been raging since the late 1940s. Thus, a gold medal won by individual athletes or teams representing one side was more of a political victory than the result of friendly competition. Each Olympics featured no shortage of off-the-field melodrama. Who would represent China, the nationalists or communists? Would the East and West Germans, bitter ideological enemies, be forced to compete as one? Would South Africa's national policy of apartheid bar that country from participating? (It did, beginning in 1964.)

Another controversial issue concerned the definition of amateur athletics. In some countries—the Soviet Union, for one—Olympic athletes were supported by the state. Yet they still were considered amateurs and were allowed to compete. American athletes did not enjoy the luxury of government support, yet once they were paid for stepping onto an athletic field they lost their amateur status and no longer could represent their country in the Olympics.

Olympic controversies were not limited to East-versus-West. In 1968, American Tommie Smith (1944–) won a gold medal in the 200-meter race; his teammate, John Carlos (1945–), finished third. During the playing of "The Star Spangled Banner," as they received their medals, both raised their black-gloved fists into the air. Smith hoisted his right one, to represent black power; Carlos raised his left, to signify unity in black America. International Olympic Committee president Avery Brundage (1887–1975) suspended them and sent them home, stripped of their medals.

❖ *SPORTS ILLUSTRATED:* EXPANDING THE SPORTS BEAT

In the 1950s and 1960s, Americans had more hours in which to indulge in their favorite pastimes. Consequently, they increasingly followed their favorite amateur and professional sports. All received coverage in local newspapers. However, a market emerged for a national sports publication that offered what local journalists could not: lengthy, detailed analyses of sporting events and sports personalities, illustrated with dramatic, full-color photos. Henry Luce (1898–1967), the editor of *Time* magazine, acknowledged this market when he initiated publication of *Sports Illustrated* (*SI*). The magazine debuted in August 1954. Milwaukee Braves third-baseman Eddie Mathews (1931–2001) was pictured on the first cover.

Initially, the magazine covered sports as well as such then-male-oriented pursuits as fishing, yachting, and big game hunting. It was not until the 1960s that *SI* became a leader in sports journalism. At that time, its editorial thrust was changed to emphasize coverage of the major sports. It also spotlighted sports-related issues, ranging from the treatment of black athletes to the increasing presence of women on playing fields.

Later, *SI* became well known for its swimsuit issues, featuring glossy photos of models in beach attire. However, during its first decades, it offered fans an entirely new way in which to read about sports.

For More Information

BOOKS

Allen, Maury. *Big-Time Baseball: A Complete Record of the National Sport.* New York: Hart Publishing Company, 1978.

Bacho, Peter. *Boxing in Black and White.* New York: Henry Holt, 1999.

Biracree, Tom. *Wilma Rudolph.* New York: Chelsea House, 1988.

Carroll, Bob, Michael Gershman, David Neff, and John Thorn, eds. *Total Football II.* New York: HarperCollins, 1999.

Center, Bill, and Bob Moore. *NASCAR Fifty Greatest Drivers.* New York: Harper-Horizon, 1998.

Christopher, Matt. *Great Moments in Baseball History.* Boston: Little, Brown & Company, 1996.

Collins, David R. *Arthur Ashe: Against the Wind.* New York: Dillon Press, 1994.

Diamond, Dan, Ralph Dinger, and James Duplacey, eds. *Total Hockey.* Kingston, NY: Total Sports, 1998.

Falla, Jack, ed. *Quest for the Cup: A History of the Stanley Cup Finals, 1893–2001.* San Diego, CA: Thunder Bay Press, 2001.

Flanagan, Alice K. *Wilma Rudolph: Athlete and Educator.* Chicago: Ferguson Publishing Company, 2000.

Gilbert, Thomas. *Pete Rose.* New York: Chelsea House, 1995.

Gilbert, Thomas. *Roberto Clemente.* New York: Chelsea House, 1991.

Greenspan, Bud. *100 Greatest Moments in Olympic History.* Los Angeles: General Publishing Group, 1995

Gutman, Bill. *The Kids' World Almanac of Basketball.* Mahwah, NJ: World Almanac Books, 1995.

Heinz, W.C., and Nathan Ward, eds. *The Book of Boxing.* New York: Total Sports, 1999.

Hubbard, Jan, ed. *The Official NBA Encyclopedia, Third Edition.* New York: Doubleday, 2000.

Myers, Walter Dean. *The Greatest: Muhammad Ali.* New York: Scholastic Press, 2001.

Ritter, Lawrence. *The Story of Baseball.* Rev. ed. New York: Morrow Junior Books, 1999.

Rummel, Jack. *Muhammad Ali.* New York: Chelsea House, 1988.

Ruth, Amy. *Wilma Rudolph*. Minneapolis: Lerner Publications, 2000.

Savage, Jeff. *Home Run Kings*. Austin, TX: Raintree Steck-Vaughn, 1999.

Schoor, Gene. *Football's Greatest Coach: Vince Lombardi*. Garden City, NY: Doubleday, 1974.

Schulman, Arlene. *Muhammad Ali: Champion*. Minneapolis: Lerner Publications, 1996.

Stewart, Mark. *Baseball: A History of the National Pastime*. New York: Franklin Watts, 1998.

Stewart, Mark. *Basketball: A History of Hoops*. New York: Franklin Watts, 1999.

Stewart, Mark. *Football: A History of the Gridiron Game*. New York: Franklin Watts, 1998.

Tessitore, John. *Muhammad Ali: The World's Champion*. New York: Franklin Watts, 1998.

Thorn, John, Pete Palmer, and Michael Gershman, eds. *Total Baseball, Seventh Edition*. Kingston, NY: Total Sports, 2001.

Whittingham, Richard. *Rites of Autumn: The Story of College Football*. New York: Free Press, 2001.

Wright, David K. *Arthur Ashe: Breaking the Color Barrier in Tennis*. Springfield, NJ: Enslow Publishers, 1996.

WEB SITES

By Popular Demand: Jackie Robinson and Other Baseball Highlights, 1860s–1960s. http://memory.loc.gov/ammem/jrhtml/jrhome.html (accessed on August 6, 2002).

1960s Flashback—Sports. http://www.1960sflashback.com/1960/Sports.asp (accessed on August 6, 2002).

Who2 Profile: Muhammad Ali. http://www.who2.com/muhammadali.html (accessed on August 6, 2002).

Where to Learn More

BOOKS

Allen, Maury. *Big-Time Baseball: A Complete Record of the National Sport.* New York: Hart Publishing Company, 1978.

Allen, Zita. *Black Women Leaders of the Civil Rights Movement.* Danbury, CT: Franklin Watts, 1996.

Anderson, Christopher J. *Grunts: U.S. Infantry in Vietnam.* Philadelphia: Chelsea House, 1999.

Andryszewski, Tricia. *Abortion: Rights, Options, and Choices.* Brookfield, CT: Millbrook Press, 1996.

Andryszewski, Tricia. *Gay Rights.* Brookfield, CT: Twenty-First Century Books, 2000.

Andryszewski, Tricia. *The March on Washington, 1963: A Gathering to Be Heard.* Brookfield, CT: Millbrook Press, 1996.

Archer, Jules. *They Had a Dream: The Civil Rights Struggle from Frederick Douglas to Marcus Garvey to Martin Luther King, Jr. and Malcolm X.* New York: Viking, 1993.

Archer, Jules. *To Save the Earth: The American Environmental Movement.* New York: Viking Press, 1998.

Aronson, Marc. *Art Attack: A Short Cultural History of the Avant-Garde.* New York: Clarion Books, 1998.

Bacho, Peter. *Boxing in Black and White.* New York: Henry Holt, 1999.

Banfield, Susan. *The Fifteenth Amendment: African American Men's Right to Vote.* Springfield, NJ: Enslow Publishers, 1998.

Beck, Ken, and Jim Clark. *The Andy Griffith Show Book*. New York: St. Martin's Press, 1995.

Bergamini, Andrea. *The History of Rock Music*. Hauppauge, NY: Barron's, 2000.

Berger, Melvin. *The Artificial Heart*. New York: Franklin Watts, 1987.

Bergman, Carol. *Sidney Poitier*. New York: Chelsea House, 1989.

Bilger, Burkhard. *Global Warming (Earth at Risk)*. New York: Chelsea House, 1992.

Billings, Charlene W. *Lasers: The New Technology of Light*. New York: Facts on File, 1992.

Biracree, Tom. *Wilma Rudolph*. New York: Chelsea House, 1988.

Bode, Janet. *The Colors of Freedom: Immigrant Stories*. New York: Franklin Watts, 1999.

Boon, Kevin Alexander. *The Human Genome Project: What Does Decoding DNA Mean for Us*. Berkeley Heights, NJ: Enslow Publishers, 2002.

Breitman, George, ed. *Malcolm X Speaks: Selected Speeches and Statements*. New York: Grove Press, 1990

Brooks, Tim, and Earle Marsh. *The Complete Directory of Prime Time Network and Cable TV Shows,* 4th ed. New York: Ballantine Books, 1999.

Brooks, Tim. *The Complete Dictionary of Prime Time TV Stars*. New York: Ballantine Books, 1987.

Brubaker, Paul. *The Cuban Missile Crisis in American History*. Berkeley Heights, NJ: Enslow Publishers, 2001.

Calabro, Marian. *Zap!: A Brief History of Television*. New York: Maxwell Macmillan International, 1992.

Carroll, Bob, Michael Gershman, David Neff, and John Thorn, eds. *Total Football II*. New York: HarperCollins, 1999.

Celsi, Teresa Noel. *Jesse Jackson and Political Power*. Brookfield CT: Millbrook Press, 1991.

Celsi, Teresa Noel. *Ralph Nader: The Consumer Revolution*. Brookfield, CT: Millbrook Press, 1991.

Center, Bill, and Bob Moore. *NASCAR Fifty Greatest Drivers*. New York: Harper-Horizon, 1998.

Chafe, William H. *The Road to Equality: American Women Since 1962*. New York: Oxford University Press, 1994.

Christopher, Matt. *Great Moments in Baseball History*. Boston: Little Brown & Company, 1996.

Clayton, Lawrence, Ph.D. *Tranquilizers*. Springfield, NJ: Enslow Publishers, 1997.

Cole, Michael D. *John F. Kennedy: President of the New Frontier*. Springfield, NJ: Enslow Publishers, 1996.

Cole, Michael D. *John Glenn: Astronaut and Senator,* rev. ed. Berkeley Heights, NJ: Enslow Publishers, 2000.

Collins, David R. *Arthur Ashe: Against the Wind*. New York: Dillon Press, 1994.

Couper, Heather, and Nigel Henbest. *Big Bang: The Story of the Universe.* New York: DK Publishing, 1996.

Couper, Heather, and Nigel Henbest. *DK Space Encyclopedia.* New York: DK Publishing, 1999.

Couper, Heather, and Nigel Henbest. *The Guide to the Galaxy.* New York and Cambridge, England: Cambridge University Press, 1994.

Couper, Heather, and Nigel Henbest. *How the Universe Works.* Pleasantville, NY: Reader's Digest Association, 1994.

Couper, Heather, and Nigel Henbest. *New Worlds: In Search of the Planets.* Reading, MA: Addison-Wesley, 1985.

Currie, Stephen. *Abortion.* San Diego: Greenhaven Press, 2000.

Darby, Jean. *Dwight D. Eisenhower: A Man Called Ike.* Minneapolis: Lerner Publications, 1989.

Darby, Jean. *Martin Luther King, Jr.* Minneapolis: Lerner Publications, 1990.

Davis, Ossie. *Just Like Martin.* New York: Simon & Schuster, 1992.

Day, Nancy. *Killer Superbugs: The Story of Drug-Resistant Diseases.* Berkeley Heights, NJ: Enslow Publishers, 2001.

De Angelis, Gina. *Nicotine and Cigarettes.* Philadelphia: Chelsea House, 1999.

Diamond, Dan, Ralph Dinger, and James Duplacey, eds. *Total Hockey.* Kingston, NY: Total Sports, 1998.

Dubovoy, Sina. *Civil Rights Leaders.* New York: Facts on File, 1997.

Dudzinski, Kathleen. *Meeting Dolphins: My Adventures in the Sea.* Washington, DC: National Geographic Society, 2000.

Dukert, Joseph M. *Nuclear Ships of the World.* New York: Coward, McCann & Geoghegan, 1973.

Durrett, Deanne. *The Abortion Conflict: A Pro/Con Issue.* Berkeley Heights, NJ: Enslow Publishers, 2000.

Dyson, Marianne J. *Space Station Science: Life in Free Fall.* New York: Scholastic Trade, 1999.

Edelman, Bernard, ed. *Dear America: Letters Home From Vietnam.* New York: Norton, 1985.

Engelbert, Phyllis, ed. *Astronomy & Space: From the Big Bang to the Big Crunch.* Detroit: U•X•L, 1996.

Epstein, Dan. *The 60's (20th Century Pop Culture).* Broomall, PA: Chelsea House, 2000.

Evers, Myrlie. *For Us, the Living.* Jackson, MS: Banner Books, 1996.

Faber, Doris. *The Smithsonian Book of First Ladies: Their Lives, Times, and Issues.* New York: Henry Holt & Company, 1996.

Falla, Jack, ed. *Quest for the Cup: A History of the Stanley Cup Finals, 1893–2001.* San Diego: Thunder Bay Press, 2001.

Feinberg, Barbara Silberdick. *America's First Ladies: Changing Expectations.* New York: Franklin Watts, 1998.

Feinstein, Stephen. *The 1960s from the Vietnam War to Flower Power.* Berkeley Heights, NJ: Enslow, 2000.

Finkelstein, Norman H. *Thirteen Days/Ninety Miles: The Cuban Missile Crisis.* New York: J. Messner, 1994.

Flanagan, Alice K. *Wilma Rudolph: Athlete and Educator.* Chicago: Ferguson Publishing Company, 2000.

Ford, Carin T. *Andy Warhol: Pioneer of Pop Art.* Berkeley Heights, NJ: Enslow Publishers, 2001.

Fridell, Ron. *Global Warming.* New York: Franklin Watts, 2002.

Galas, Judith. *Gay Rights.* San Diego: Lucent Books, 1995.

Gardner, Robert. *Health Science Projects About Heredity.* Berkeley Heights, NJ: Enslow Publishers, 2001.

Gay, Kathlyn. *Pregnancy: Private Decisions, Public Debates.* New York: Franklin Watts, 1994.

Gay, Kathlyn. *Who's Running the Nation? How Corporate Power Threatens Democracy.* New York: Franklin Watts, 1998.

Gilbert, Thomas. *Pete Rose.* New York: Chelsea House, 1995.

Gilbert, Thomas. *Roberto Clemente.* New York: Chelsea House, 1991.

Gold, Susan Dudley. *Roe V. Wade: Abortion.* New York: Twenty-First Century Books, 1994.

Goldman, Martin S. *John F. Kennedy: Portrait of a President.* New York: Facts on File, 1995.

Goldman, Martin S. *Richard M. Nixon: The Complex President.* New York: Facts on File, 1998.

Gonzales, Doreen. *Cesar Chavez: Leader for Migrant Farm Workers.* Springfield, NJ: Enslow Publishers, 1996.

Gourley, Catherine. *Media Wizards: A Behind-the-Scenes Look at Media Manipulations.* Brookfield, CT: Twenty-First Century Books, 1999.

Gourse, Leslie. *Aretha Franklin: Lady Soul.* New York: Franklin Watts, 1995.

Grant, R. G. *The Sixties.* Austin, TX: Raintree/Steck-Vaughn, 2000.

Green, Robert. *John Glenn: Astronaut and U.S. Senator.* Chicago: Ferguson Publishing, 2001.

Greenberg, Cara. *Up to Pop: Furniture in the 1960s.* Boston: Little Brown & Company, 1999.

Greenspan, Bud. *100 Greatest Moments in Olympic History.* Los Angeles: General Publishing Group, 1995.

Guernsey, Joann Bren. *Voices of Feminism: Past, Present, and Future.* Minneapolis: Lerner Publications, 1996.

Gutman, Bill. *The Kids' World Almanac of Basketball*. Mahwah, NJ: World Almanac Books, 1995.

Haley, James, ed. *Global Warming: Opposing Viewpoints*. San Diego: Greenhaven Press, 2002.

Halliwell, Sarah, ed. *The 20th Century: Post-1945 Artists, Writers, and Composers*. Austin, TX: Raintree/Steck-Vaughn, 1998.

Hampton, Wilborn. *Kennedy Assassinated! The World Mourns: A Reporter's Story*. Cambridge, MA: Candlewick Press, 1997.

Haskins, James. *Separate, but Not Equal: The Dream and the Struggle*. New York: Scholastic, 1998.

Hay, Jeff, ed. *Richard Nixon*. San Diego: Greenhaven Press, 2001.

Heinz, W. C., and Nathan Ward, eds. *The Book of Boxing*. New York: Total Sports, 1999.

Henricksson, John. *Rachel Carson: The Environmental Movement*. Brookfield, CT: Millbrook Press, 1991.

Herda, D. J. *Roe V. Wade: The Abortion Question*. Hillside, NJ: Enslow Publishers, 1994.

Holland, Gini. *The 1960s*. San Diego, CA: Lucent, 1999.

Holmes, Burnham. *Cesar Chavez: Farm Worker Activist*. Austin, TX: Raintree/ Steck-Vaughn, 1994.

Horwitz, Elinor Lander. *On the Land: American Agriculture from Past to Present*. New York: Atheneum, 1980.

Hubbard, Jan, ed. *The Official NBA Encyclopedia, Third Edition*. New York: Doubleday, 2000.

Hurley, Jennifer A., ed. *Feminism: Opposing Viewpoints*. San Diego: Greenhaven Press, 2000.

Ingram, Philip. *Russia and the USSR: 1905–1991*. Cambridge, England: Cambridge University Press, 1997.

Jezer, Marty. *Rachel Carson*. New York: Chelsea House, 1988.

Johnson, Rebecca L. *The Greenhouse Effect: Life on a Warmer Planet*. Minneapolis: Lerner Publications, 1993.

Judson, Karen. *The Presidency of the United States*. Springfield, NJ: Enslow Publishers, 1996.

Kallen, Stuart A., ed. *Sixties Counterculture*. San Diego: Greenhaven Press, 2000.

Katz, Ephraim. *The Film Encyclopedia*, 4th ed. New York: HarperResource, 2001.

Knapp, Ron. *American Legends of Rock*. Springfield, NJ: Enslow Publishers, 1996.

Kort, Michael. *China Under Communism*. Brookfield, CT: Millbrook Press, 1994.

Kort, Michael. *The Cold War*. Brookfield, CT: Millbrook Press, 1994.

Kort, Michael. *Russia*. New York: Facts on File, 1995.

Krafsur, Richard, exec. ed. *The American Film Institute Catalog of Motion Pictures, Feature Films, 1961–1970.* New York: R. Bowker, 1976.

Kramer, Barbara. *Neil Armstrong: The First Man on the Moon.* Springfield, NJ: Enslow Publishers, 1997.

Kramer, Barbara. *Ron Howard: Child Star & Hollywood Director.* Springfield, NJ: Enslow Publishers, 1998.

Kroc, Ray, with Robert Anderson. *Grinding It Out: The Making of McDonald's.* Chicago: H. Regnery, 1977.

Lambert, Lisa A. *The Leakeys.* Vero Beach, FL: Roarke Publishers, 1993.

Landau, Elaine. *John F. Kennedy, Jr.* Brookfield, CT: Twenty-First Century Books, 2000.

Lassieur, Allison. *Abortion.* San Diego: Lucent Books, 2001.

Love, John F. *McDonald's: Behind the Arches.* New York: Bantam Books, 1986.

Lowenstein, Felicia. *The Abortion Battle: Looking at Both Sides.* Springfield, NJ: Enslow Publishers, 1996.

Lusane, Clarence. *No Easy Victories: Black Americans and the Vote.* New York: Franklin Watts, 1996.

Lusane, Clarence. *The Struggle for Equal Education.* New York: Franklin Watts, 1992.

Malatesta, Anne, and Ronald Friedland. *The White Kikuya: Louis S.B. Leakey.* New York: McGraw-Hill, 1978.

Maltin, Leonard, ed. *Leonard Maltin's Movie Encyclopedia.* New York: Dutton, 1994.

Maltin, Leonard, ed. *Movie & Video Guide,* 22nd ed. New York: Signet, 2001.

Martin, Marvin. *The Beatles: The Music Was Never the Same.* New York: Franklin Watts, 1996.

McNeil, Alex. *Total Television,* 4th ed. New York: Penguin Books, 1996.

Mills, Judie. *John F. Kennedy.* New York: Franklin Watts, 1988.

Mills, Judie. *Robert Kennedy.* Brookfield, CT: Millbrook Press, 1998.

Morgan, Sally. *Smoking.* Austin, TX: Raintree/Steck-Vaughn, 2002.

Myers, Walter Dean. *The Greatest: Muhammad Ali.* New York: Scholastic Press, 2001.

Myers, Walter Dean. *Malcolm X: By Any Means Necessary.* New York: Scholastic Paperbacks, 1993.

Nardo, Don. *Lasers: Humanity's Magic Light.* San Diego: Lucent Books, 1990.

Netzley, Patricia D. *Issues in the Environment.* San Diego, Lucent Books, 1998.

Northrup, Mary. *American Computer Pioneers.* Springfield, NJ: Enslow Publishers, 1998.

O'Connell, Arthur J. *American Business in the 20th Century.* San Mateo, CA: Bluewood Books, 1999.

Olian, JoAnne, ed. *Everyday Fashions of the Sixties, as Pictured in Sears Catalogs.* Mineola, NY: Dover Publications, 1999.

Oliver, Marilyn Tower. *Gay and Lesbian Rights: A Struggle.* Springfield, NJ: Enslow Publications, 1998.

Pietrusza, David. *John F. Kennedy.* San Diego: Lucent Books, 1997.

Pogue, William R. *How Do You Go to the Bathroom in Space?*, rev. ed. New York: Tom Doherty Associates, 1999.

Powe-Temperley, Kitty. *The 60s: Mods & Hippies.* Milwaukee, WI: Gareth Stevens, 2000.

Poynter, Margaret. *The Leakeys: Uncovering the Origins of Humankind.* Springfield, NJ: Enslow Publishers, 1997.

Pringle, Laurence. *The Environmental Movement: From Its Roots to the Challenges of a New Century.* New York: HarperCollins Juvenile Books, 2000.

Pringle, Laurence. *Smoking: A Risky Business.* New York: Morrow Junior Books, 1996.

Rasmussen, R. Kent. *Farewell Jim Crow: The Rise and Fall of Segregation in America.* New York: Facts on File, 1997.

Ritter, Lawrence. *The Story of Baseball,* rev. ed. New York: Morrow Junior Books, 1999.

Robbins, Ocean, and Sol Solomon. *Choices for Our Future: A Generation Rising for Life.* Summertown, TN: Book Pub Co., 1994.

Roleff, Tamara L., ed. *Abortion: Opposing Viewpoints.* San Diego: Greenhaven Press, 1997.

Roleff, Tamara, ed. *Gay Rights.* San Diego: Greenhaven Press, 1996.

Roleff, Tamara, ed. *Global Warming: Opposing Viewpoints.* San Diego: Greenhaven Press, 1997.

Roleff, Tamara L., and Mary E. Williams, eds. *Tobacco and Smoking: Opposing Viewpoints.* San Diego: Greenhaven Press, 1998.

Romaine, Deborah H. *Roe V. Wade: Abortion and the Supreme Court.* San Diego: Lucent Books, 1998.

Rummel, Jack. *Muhammad Ali.* New York: Chelsea House, 1988.

Ruth, Amy. *Wilma Rudolph.* Minneapolis: Lerner Publications, 2000.

Savage, Jeff. *Home Run Kings.* Austin, TX: Raintree/Steck-Vaughn, 1999.

Schoor, Gene. *Football's Greatest Coach: Vince Lombardi.* Garden City, NY: Doubleday, 1974.

Schraff, Anne E. *Coretta Scott King: Striving for Civil Rights.* Springfield, NJ: Enslow Publishers, 1997.

Schulman, Arlene. *Muhammad Ali: Champion.* Minneapolis: Lerner Publications, 1996.

Schuman, Michael. *Bill Cosby: Actor and Comedian.* Springfield, NJ: Enslow Publishers, 1995.

Where to Learn More

Schuman, Michael. *Lyndon B. Johnson.* Springfield, NJ: Enslow Publishers, 1998.

Schuman, Michael. *Martin Luther King, Jr.: Leader for Civil Rights.* Springfield, NJ: Enslow Publishers, 1996.

Schwager, Tina, and Michele Schuerger. *Gutsy Girls: Young Women Who Dare.* Minneapolis: Free Spirit Publishing, 1999.

Sharpe, Mitchell R. *"It Is I, Sea Gull": Valentina Tereshkova, First Woman in Space.* New York: Crowell, 1975.

Sheafer, Silvia Anne. *Aretha Franklin: Motown Superstar.* Springfield, NJ: Enslow Publishers, 1996.

Shirley, David. *The History of Rock & Roll.* New York: Franklin Watts, 1987.

Siegel, Beatrice. *Murder on the Highway: The Viola Liuzzo Story.* New York: Four Winds Press, 1993.

Silver, Diane. *The New Civil War: The Lesbian and Gay Struggle for Civil Rights.* New York: Franklin Watts, 1997.

Silverstein, Alvin, Virginia Silverstein, and Robert Silverstein. *Measles and Rubella.* Springfield, NJ: Enslow Publishers, 1997.

Smith, Howard E. *Daring the Unknown: A History of NASA.* San Diego: Harcourt Brace Jovanovich, 1987.

Soto, Gary. *Jessie De La Cruz: A Profile of a United Farm Worker.* New York: Persea Books, 2000.

Southard, Andy. *Hot Rods and Custom Cars of the 1960s.* Osceola, WI: Motorbooks International, 1997.

Spangenburg, Ray, and Diane K. Moser. *Living and Working in Space.* New York: Facts on File, 1989.

Spangenburg, Ray, and Diane K. Moser. *Opening the Space Frontier.* New York: Facts on File, 1989.

Spangenburg, Ray, and Diane K. Moser. *Space Exploration: Exploring the Reaches of the Solar System.* New York: Facts on File, 1990.

Spangenburg, Ray, and Kit Moser. *Artificial Satellites.* New York: Franklin Watts, 2001.

Spangenburg, Ray, and Kit Moser. *History of NASA.* New York: Franklin Watts, 2000.

Spangenburg, Ray, and Kit Moser. *Project Apollo.* New York: Franklin Watts, 2001.

Spangenburg, Ray, and Kit Moser. *Project Gemini.* New York: Franklin Watts, 2001.

Spangenburg, Ray, and Kit Moser. *Project Mercury.* New York: Franklin Watts, 2001.

Stefoff, Rebecca. *The American Environmental Movement.* New York: Facts on File, 1995.

Stewart, Mark. *Basketball: A History of Hoops.* New York: Franklin Watts, 1999.

Stewart, Mark. *Baseball: A History of the National Pastime.* New York: Franklin Watts, 1998.

Stewart, Mark. *Football: A History of the Gridiron Game.* New York: Franklin Watts, 1998.

Streissguth, Tom. *John Glenn.* Minneapolis: Lerner Publications, 1999.

Strong, Susan. *The Greatness of Girls: Famous Women Talk About Growing Up.* Kansas City: Andrews McMeel, 2001.

Stwertka, Albert, and Eve Stwertka. *Physics: From Newton to the Big Bang.* New York: Franklin Watts, 1986.

Terry, Luther L., and Daniel Horn. *To Smoke or Not to Smoke.* New York: Lothrop Lee & Shepard, 1969.

Tesar, Jenny. *Global Warming.* New York: Facts on File, 1991.

Tessitore, John. *Muhammad Ali: The World's Champion.* New York: Franklin Watts, 1998.

Thorn, John, Pete Palmer, and Michael Gershman, eds. *Total Baseball,* 7th ed. Kingston, NY: Total Sports, 2001.

Thro, Ellen. *Robotics: The Marriage of Computers and Machines.* New York, Facts on File, 1993.

Vaughan, William H. T. *Encyclopedia of Artists.* New York: Oxford University Press, 2000.

Vernell, Marjorie. *Leaders of Black Civil Rights.* San Diego: Lucent Books, 2000.

Vogt, Gregory. *Apollo and the Moon Landing.* Brookfield, CT: Millbrook Press, 1991.

Vogt, Gregory. *John Glenn's Return to Space.* Brookfield, CT: Millbrook Press, 2000.

Vogt, Gregory. *The Solar System: Facts and Exploration.* New York: Twenty-First Century Books, 1995.

Vogt, Gregory. *The Space Shuttle: Missions in Space.* Brookfield, CT: Millbrook Press, 1991.

Vogt, Gregory. *A Twenty-Fifth Anniversary Album of NASA.* New York: Franklin Watts, 1983.

Waldman, Allison J. *The Barbra Streisand Scrapbook.* Secaucus, NJ: Citadel Press, 1995.

Waldron, Vince. *The Official Dick Van Dyke Show Book.* New York: Hyperion, 1994.

Walter, Mildred Pitts. *Mississippi Challenge.* New York: Bradbury Press, 1992.

Weiss, Malcolm E. *Man Explores the Sea.* New York: J. Messner, 1969.

Whittingham, Richard. *Rites of Autumn: The Story of College Football.* New York: Free Press, 2001.

Williams, Mary E., ed. *Abortion: Opposing Viewpoints.* San Diego: Greenhaven Press, 2001.

Where to Learn More

Willis, Delta. *The Leakey Family: Leaders in the Search for Human Origins.* New York: Facts on File, 1992.

Winkler, Allan M. *The Cold War: A History in Documents.* New York: Oxford University Children's Books, 2001.

Wright, David K. *Arthur Ashe: Breaking the Color Barrier in Tennis.* Springfield, NJ: Enslow Publishers, 1996.

Wright, David K. *John Lennon: The Beatles and Beyond.* Springfield, NJ: Enslow Publishers, 1996.

WEB SITES

An American Cultural History: 1960–1969. http://www.nhmccd.edu/contracts/lrc/kc/decade60.html (accessed on August 12, 2002).

Bilingual Education. http://ourworld.compuserve.com/homepages/JWCRAWFORD/biling.htm (accessed on August 6, 2002).

Biographies: Louis Leakey. http://www.talkorigins.org/faqs/homs/lleakey.html (accessed on August 6, 2002).

British Sports Cars vs. American Sports Cars During the 1960s and 1970s. http://www.geocities.com/pattonr1_04011/Sportscars.html (accessed on August 6, 2002).

By Popular Demand: Jackie Robinson and Other Baseball Highlights, 1860s–1960s. http://memory.loc.gov/ammem/jrhtml/jrhome.html (accessed on August 6, 2002).

The Conservative 1960s. http://www.theatlantic.com/issues/95dec/conbook/conbook.htm (accessed on August 6, 2002).

Fashion Flashbacks. http://www.fashion-flashbacks.com/20cen/20cen1960s.html (accessed on August 6, 2002).

Greatest Space Events of the 20th Century: The 60s. http://www.space.com/news/spacehistory/greatest_space_events_1960s.html (accessed on August 6, 2002).

John F. Kennedy. http://www.americanpresident.org/kotrain/courses/JFK/JFK_The_American_Franchise.htm (accessed on August 6, 2002).

Lyndon B. Johnson. http://www.americanpresident.org/kotrain/courses/LBJ/LBJ_In_Brief.htm (accessed on August 6, 2002).

The Man Who Saved Your Life—Maurice R. Hilleman. http://www.njabr.org/superstars/hilleman/hilleman8.cfm (accessed on August 6, 2002).

1960s Flashback—Economy/Prices. http://www.1960sflashback.com/1960/Economy.asp (accessed on August 6, 2002).

1960s Flashback—1960's Movies. http://www.1960sflashback.com/1960/Movies.asp (accessed on August 12, 2002).

1960s Flashback—Potpourri. http://www.1960sflashback.com/1960/Potpourri.asp (accessed on August 6, 2002).

1960s Flashback—Sports. http://www.1960sflashback.com/1960/Sports.asp (accessed on August 6, 2002).

1960s Flashback—TV. http://www.1960sflashback.com/1960/TV.asp (accessed on August 12, 2002).

Peace Corps. http://www.peacecorps.gov/about/history/decades//60s.cfm (accessed on August 6, 2002).

Planned Parenthood Federation of America—1960s. http://member.planned parenthood.org/site/PageServer?pagename=1960s (accessed on August 6, 2002).

Vietnam War and the 1960s. http://www.geocities.com/Athens/Forum/9235/vet. html (accessed on August 6, 2002).

Who2 Profile: Muhammad Ali. http://www.who2.com/muhammadali.html (accessed on August 6, 2002).

Women in Folk Music—Female Singers and Songwriters. http://womenshistory .about.com/cs/musicfolk/ (accessed on August 6, 2002).

The Women's Health Movement from the 1960s to the Present, and Beyond. http://www.4woman.gov/owh/pub/history/healthmvmt.htm (accessed on August 6, 2002).

Index